MW00358807

I, *Witness*

JOSEPH A. MCGEE

ISBN 978-1-0980-4197-7 (paperback)
ISBN 978-1-0980-4198-4 (hardcover)
ISBN 978-1-0980-4199-1 (digital)

Copyright © 2020 by Joseph A. McGee

All rights reserved. No part of this publication may be reproduced, distributed, or transmitted in any form or by any means, including photocopying, recording, or other electronic or mechanical methods without the prior written permission of the publisher. For permission requests, solicit the publisher via the address below.

Christian Faith Publishing, Inc.
832 Park Avenue
Meadville, PA 16335
www.christianfaithpublishing.com

All scripture quotations, unless otherwise indicated, are taken from the Holy Bible, New International Version®, NIV® Copyright ©1973, 1978, 1984, 2011 by Biblica, Inc.™ Used by permission of Zondervan. All rights reserved worldwide. www.Zondervan.com. The "NIV" and "New International Version" are trademarks registered in the United States Patent and Trademark Office by Biblica, Inc. (TM).

Printed in the United States of America

DEDICATION

This book is dedicated to the outsiders, the throwaways, the outcasts, the prisoners and all the other people society disowns.

> *But God chose the foolish things of the world to shame the wise; God chose the weak things of the world to shame the strong. God chose the lowly things and the despised things—and the things that are not—to nullify the things that are, so that no one may boast before him.* (1 Cor. 1:27–28)

Also, all royalties from this book will go to the shelter where I volunteer.

Thanks to my beautiful wife for putting up with me, and to my church friends for all their help and inspiration.

And thanks to God, from whom all blessings flow.

Contents

FOREWORD

This writing is autobiographical, but it is not an autobiography. I have included enough details about myself and my life for the reader to get a picture of who I am, for perspective, and to better understand what it is that happened that I felt compelled to write about. All of these things in my life are true and none are made up or embellished, but I have intentionally shortened the story, so as to get to the point as expeditiously as possible. A lot is left out, intentionally.

I want to be clear that none of these things happened because I am a good person. I have been tormented for years over some of my doings, and but for Christ's blood, I would be so bedeviled now.

But Christ did not die on a cross for saints, but for sinners. It is for our sins, that Yeshua (Jesus's name in Hebrew) died.

I can tell you honestly and truly, some of the most Christian people I ever met were saved IN PRISON. In a cold cell, behind iron bars with a cot, toilet and sink of stainless steel, alone to contemplate their lives. Thusly, Jesus Christ found them, and redeemed them. Some had been very serious criminals, gangsters, even murderers. Yet Jesus thought they were worth dying for. And they are not worse people than you or I.

Christ saves all and no one can boast before God. (1 Cor. 1:29)

It was as a lone sinner, dying of cancer, and carrying the burden of guilt, that Christ found me. It was by His grace, and His grace alone, that He showed me mercy, and because I believed, He saved me from my sin.

I. LIFE BEFORE CANCER

It is hard sometimes to remember how I felt then, so much has happened since. For thirty years I was a lawyer. First with a private firm and later with an insurance company, I defended and tried cases, mostly civil, in all kinds of courts, state and federal. I celebrated victories and suffered defeats. I made brilliant arguments and abysmal mistakes. I rode a roller coaster of emotions with every case.

I did love trials, but honestly, most of my time was in the office. The way cases are won, in my experience, is by spending countless hours poring over documents, evidence, interrogatories and deposition transcripts looking for the minute details that help to counter the arguments of the other side, and build up one's own theory of the case. From these one gradually constructs a theme, something catchy, and uses it in opening and closing argument and in the examination of every witness. One carefully plots cross examinations to force hostile witnesses to admit the details that support one's case or refute theirs. Show me a brilliant lawyer in the courtroom and I'll show you a drudge, huddled over his files in the office, burning the midnight oil. This may be part of the reason depression, addiction and suicide rates for lawyers are well above the national average.

2. MY STRANGE CHILDHOOD

Everyone's formative years have much to do with the adult that they become, so in order for you to understand my vision and my message, I am telling you first about myself. Whatever led me on such a tortuous journey had to have begun then. There were things that happened that should never have happened. Honestly, some of them were abusive; I suffered from a form of childhood PTSD for years. When I state that, I mean I had flashbacks in response to triggering events, abnormal fears, nightmares and parts of memories that were blacked out. In other words, certain classic symptoms. But they were things I was able to work around as I got older, and as I grew to adulthood, these symptoms were compensated for. I was able to just avoid certain things, and overcome others. For example, I politely declined when my friends suggested I try skydiving.

Also, I had no normal early childhood socialization with other kids my age. Most children learn by the age of four how to socialize and get along with other children. Today, we know that this early socialization is important for "normal" development. I knew there were other children, but I never really met any until I was in school. And even then, I saw them in school. I had no other interaction, no visiting one another's homes for play, no sleepovers.

When I was very little we lived in a dingy gray apartment on the third floor of a building with no elevators. I didn't like it very much, because it was big and cold and dusty. I was alone there with my mother a lot. She always seemed sad. I had no idea why, nor did I think it strange at the time. When you are little, you accept life as normal. I now know for example, that I had a half-sister, born to her out-of-wedlock and given up for adoption. Why, I don't know, perhaps my father insisted. He was an insecure person. Perhaps, the sadness was over the biological father. Did my mother love him?

She once stated that she "should have married" a different man than my father. I was perhaps four. She was reading to me from a book by Dr. Seuss. I don't recall what brought up the subject. I have, on occasion, wondered whether my father was my biological father. We were so different; we don't look at all alike. He died at fifty-two.

Before I started school, I had no friends. I wasn't allowed outside without my mother. I remember sitting up at night with her watching TV. We watched "The Count of Monte Cristo" many times on the black and white TV.

Once, after we had moved to a house in a quiet neighborhood, I disobeyed and went out the back gate. There were some boys in the alley and they talked me into coming out. I guess I was five, they were perhaps a year or two older. They got me to the end of the alley, but I didn't want to go farther. One, who may have been the "leader," said "show him the persuader." The persuader was a piece of two by two with a nail in the end and a coiled spring around that. It looked pretty scary. My mother then emerged and ran them off.

My parents did once send me to a Boys Club day camp for a week. Most of the time I was there, I sat by myself and didn't talk to people. I did not understand what was going on or the purpose of it. Once we did go to the beach. I was sitting alone on the sand. I had no direct experience of the ocean. One of the men must have felt sorry for me. He picked me up and took me into the water. This did not enlighten me, because I was scared of the waves. I did kind of like the camp, however. The last day, they all sang "For He's a Jolly Good Fellow" to the leader. I liked that, actually. Everyone seemed happy. But I never got much out of it.

I went to kindergarten while we lived in the same place, the first and only house my parents ever owned together. It was in a quiet neighborhood. We had modern furniture and a car. I had new clothes and toys. My first school was a short walk. My mom would pack a lunch. All my sandwiches contained mayonnaise. She put it on cheese, bologna, and peanut butter. I do not think these are great combinations, but as a five-year-old, you don't have much to compare to.

School was strange for me. I was always odd man out, since the other kids had cliques or groups that knew each other, and I was the only one who knew no one, or that is how it seemed. Also, activities like music and dancing were hard for me because I was shy, never having been around kids much. I did really like the smell of the crayons. No other crayons ever smelled quite the same. This is the most positive memory I have of kindergarten.

When I was six, my family left the big city and moved to a small town in the Midwest. I remember a few days when my mother and I were in a hotel during the move. I remember sitting at the window with my mother. Everything was gray. I got a toy "space gun." It made loud bleeping noises and lit up when I pulled the trigger. It looked like something in a Buck Rodgers movie.

We rode in an airplane to our new home. It was a prop plane, since this was in the early fifties. I got motion sickness, threw up in a paper bag. I felt miserable, but it was something to fly in an airplane in those days. This was before I developed my fear of heights, which I will explain later.

The move came shortly after I had started first grade. We were forced to move in with my paternal grandparents, into a large second floor apartment. I had to go to a new school. Everything was strange.

The reason for the changes was my father's radical political views. Left wing advocates and political radicals were always tolerated in the city before, but in the early fifties, they were suddenly *persona non grata*. Not only did my father lose his job, he was blacklisted so he could not work anywhere. So now in a small town in the middle of the country, he had to start a business where nobody knew us. I am sure that was hard for him. He had been on a very good career path as an electrical engineer. I know my mother had a very hard time accepting that we were going to be relatively poor. They fought a lot. She got very emotional sometimes, and I am sure it was partly caused by the decline in economic circumstances. He would become very angry.

I was not an immediate success in the new school. I came in the middle of the school year. In fact I had a struggle adjusting. I did like the two-block walk to the school. Sometimes my grandfather walked with me. He didn't talk a lot, but he was nice. I liked him. I had a harder time with the kids. They were not very accepting at first.

My favorite book at that time was *All About Dinosaurs* by Roy Chapman Andrews. I knew all the names of all the dinosaurs, how they lived, what they ate, where the bones were found. I made clay models of them and talked about them a lot. My mom thought I should take them to school and show the class. I happily told all about them, as I had the book largely memorized. The teacher was impressed. They asked me to show them to the older class.

I was proud and began lecturing about them and passing them around. The older boys in the class, however, destroyed them. They were modeling clay, so I could make them again, but I could not understand the reason for their action. Were they not also interested in these things? Why was I rejected? My mom said it was because the boys were mean. But why would they be mean? She said that's just the way boys were, but it made no sense to me. If boys are just mean, why wasn't I mean?

The truth is that no one is naturally mean. We learn to be mean from other people. Sometimes my father was mean. I held that against him for years, but I now forgive it. He didn't set out one day to become a mean person, but life dealt him hard blows and he responded the way he did. When life deals us hardship, we have to respond by growing or contracting. In brainpower, he grew; in spirit, he contracted. He had been sick and missed a year of school at age thirteen, and was left with a physical disability. He became interested in science. What else went through his brain during that year and as he matured, we have no idea. He never shared much.

I can say he was very insecure. He especially did not like to be challenged in any way. Once, when I was three or four, and he was teasing me, I started to become angry, as children do if you tease them too long and will not relent. You can tease a kid for a while and it is great fun, but past a certain point, they become angry. Of course, he was having fun and would not stop. I had this little cowboy hat such as a kid that age might have, a toy. At one point, I was so frustrated I threw it at him. It hit a lamp. Later, I showed my mother the bruises from the belt whipping he'd given me. I blacked out the memory of the whipping, but I remember the welts on my arms and legs.

I certainly was not the only boy who ever got a whipping. But I was too young and had no experience to relate to it. The main thing was that I had never had anyone be angry that way at me before. I was terrified, and felt like he was going to kill me. I screamed as he came towering over me taking off his belt. He said, "Your mother's not around to protect you now!" Then, whatever occurred was blacked out, so I have never remembered it. I associate the incident with fear, not pain. I cannot recall any pain, just terror. I have since seen this scene play over and over again many times.

I don't tell this story to make you feel sorry for me, but just so you can understand what my life and my relationship with my father was like. Another time, I lost my two front teeth. I had insisted on trying the "big" swings at the park, the ones older kids swing on, rather than the "safe" kid swings. This was when I was with my father. Because I argued with him, he "taught me a lesson" by pushing me higher and higher, no matter my screams of terror. I was screaming "STOP!" He said "you wanted to try the big swings. Now you're trying them." He kept pushing me higher and higher. He said "hold on. Don't let go," as he pushed me harder. Finally, terrified, I let go and woke up at home on the couch without those teeth. After that I always had a fear of heights, and of falling. The weird part is, I was afraid if I got too close, I would jump or let go. Then I would feel like I did that time on the swing.

I never knew when that side of him would come out. I expected punishment when I disobeyed, but sometimes I had not disobeyed.

He wasn't always like that. Sometimes he would be nice. Sometimes I really liked him. But over the years of my childhood, there was an accumulation of resentment that was from his angry temper, his outbursts and his kind of belittling humor. Whatever devils inhabited him, he did not talk about. I felt that his belittling was always directed at me. I never heard him belittle anyone else. It made me feel ashamed, like there was something wrong with me.

So when people were mean at school, my young mind took meanness to be the way of the world. Since we had no religion, what else would I have thought? I felt that people were mean, and if one wanted to be on any kind of even footing, one would have to be mean as well.

There was another strange part of my childhood that I need to explain. When I started school, and even by the first grade, I had never thrown a baseball or a football; I had never ridden a bicycle or run a footrace. I was a weak, soft, timid boy. Also, I had no real socialization with other kids, as I stated, until I started school. So I was not only weak, I was also asocial. There was no reason for anyone to like me. I didn't know how to play.

I hated school. My first grade teacher wanted me to learn to write using my right hand. I was terrible at it. It never felt right. The pencil would not go the way I wanted, my letters were poor. She seemed to feel left-handedness was a hallmark of sin.

My worst subject was arithmetic, my father's favorite. He was Phi Beta Kappa with a triple major in math, chemistry and physics. He once sat me down because I was failing arithmetic. He said, "Now, you are going to learn this." He hit my hand with a ruler. He asked problems. He hit for wrong answers. I refused to give right answers; we were yelling at each other. When my mother tried to intervene, he said "I will not have a mathematical jackass for a son." Things at school were not much better. I was bullied because I was weak and weird, and the teachers yelled at me a lot. I was a mess.

I saw no problem with stealing, lying. We were poor at this time, I had little. I learned to self-justify. I hoarded and hid money. Not having any Christian ideas, I didn't care about sin or idolatry. What would a boy of six or seven know about these things, unless he had been taught? My parents said stealing and lying were "wrong," but they never said why.

I was also mean to my sister when I felt especially bad because of the treatment I got at school. I felt guilty about it later, but as I said, my life was a mess. I had a lot of anxiety, but I didn't know what anxiety was. To me it was just the way I felt. I am sorry for all the things I did, but cannot change the fact they happened.

I did have a couple of friends. One was an elderly lady who lived in a house next door to our back yard, separated by a chain-link fence. She invited me onto the porch and gave me something to eat and ice tea. She was very kind and I think she felt sorry for me. Once she even took me to the zoo.

There was also a boy named Tommy who lived on the other side of our building. I think he was a year younger. We used to play every day, and we really enjoyed it. I don't think he had many friends either. Then there was the peak of the polio epidemic one summer, and my mother wouldn't let me go outside, even to play with Tommy, until the day we all had to go up to the school and stand in line for the polio shot. Everyone had to go, or be banned from the public school.

Later, when I was in the fourth grade, we moved again to a rented house in another town. My parents did a strange thing. They sent my sister and me to church. Not took, *sent*. On Easter, my mother would dress up and take my sister and me. They wore white gloves. The rest of the time, we mostly went alone. My parents put on some of the trappings of "Christianity," vicariously. My father never attended. I guess he could be called many things, but he wasn't a hypocrite.

In fact, my father would argue when, as could have been predicted, we came home talking about whatever we learned in Sunday school. He would say "there is no God. Religion is the opium of the masses." He thought religion was just a salve for the "ignorant." He derided the people where we lived; he thought they were mostly ignorant "hillbillies." In fact, he talked about that subject a lot. He felt superior to those who did not have a college education.

My father revered science and mathematics. He liked to talk about scientific support for the theory of evolution. He thought evolution would refute the existence of God. He thought the theory of the Big Bang refuted the existence of God. (Actually, I don't think either statement is true. The Bible states that God created the heavens and the earth "in the beginning" (Gen. 1:1). Human beings have interpreted that in various ways. The exact date, and how God did what He did are not explicitly stated, and I refrain from expressing my opinion. My personal witness bears on the Risen Christ *only*. I am far more concerned that everyone should believe *in Him* than what they think about anything else.

Father, however, would continue in his tirades to relate the history of all the atrocities committed by sinful men in the name of religion. He could talk about the Crusades, the Inquisitions; and of the missionaries in some places, who pretended to represent Christ, while impregnating native women.

He would point out the hypocrisy of those who worship with their mouths on Sunday, and still continue to sin all week. As it is written: *"God's name is blasphemed among the gentiles because of you."* (Romans 2:24). Partly because I had been set to a nature of rebelling against his meanness, I argued back. I know that it is wrong to not honor one's parent, but when parents do not honor God, I think it is better to take the side of God.

Through all this, some of the teaching of the church stuck. I may not have understood repentance, but I at least felt guilt. What good is guilt? Guilt is a warning that something is wrong, a bread crumb on the road to repentance. I think also the example of Jesus made me less bitter and mean myself.

3. Mean and Evil

When I was a small boy, age eight or nine, my father, in a good mood (he was capable of being in a good mood), took me to see a movie. Since he told me I could choose, I picked the one I wanted to see. He tried to talk me out of it, but I insisted and he had promised. It was a really bad horror movie about a teenage "werewolf." The main character was an older teenager, maybe seventeen or so, who didn't get along well with his father and had no mother. He was (predictably) bitten by a wolf. Most of the movie was about him as he was horrified by the fact he was turning into a wolf. This made a lasting impression on my young mind. It was not as much the scariness of the wolf, but more the struggle within the boy.

My fears at night alone in my bed were of the boy and his struggle, knowing he was turning into an evil wolf, but powerless to change his destiny. I lay in the dark, staring at my hands, wondering if fur and claws would start to grow. I was horrified by the possibility that a person, not wanting to become a wolf, would turn into a monstrous and murderous wolf. This persisted for years. I'm sure some child psychologist would have fun with that one.

However, it is in fact how I think of human evil. The potential for evil, I think is present in every human heart, dormant, and waiting for something to bring it to fruition. The first pair, Adam and Eve, delved into the "godlike" knowledge of good and evil, and blood followed, as their firstborn child murdered his own brother. Blood follows sin and sin paves the way for blood. I'm not speaking as a theologian, but as a rational person who believes the Bible. Adam had no sin before the fall, but he had the potential to disobey God; with the knowledge, evil entered the world.

Many people, with good reason, think Hitler was an antichrist. And that is certainly possible; I am not saying it is wrong. The more frightening *possibility* is that he started out just like you and me. His picture, as a small child, can be viewed online. His baby pictures and childhood pictures look much like any other child. His father was described as cold, abusive and aloof; his mother a mouse. His brother, whom he loved, died when he was twelve. He became morose and detached. His father was abusive, especially when Adolf became interested in art.

(NOTE: This is NOT going to be an apology for Hitler,[1] or the other mean, evil people of the world. It is part of my own searching into the roots of *my own inner evil.* Each person is answerable to God for his own deeds (Jn. 5:29, Jer. 31:30). The Holocaust is one of the greatest atrocities in history. It cannot be denied or forgotten.)

Hitler wanted to be an artist, but his father would not hear of it. After his father's death, he left on his own to go to Vienna, hoping to be accepted to the art academy there. He was generally good, and did very nice drawings of landscapes and buildings, but could not draw faces. Maybe it was a mental block, like the one I had as a child with mathematics, a result of parental cruelty. Not willing to go home, he remained on the streets of Vienna, struggling to survive and pursue his dream. He was given employment and help at one time by a friend, who as fate would have it, was Jewish. Nevertheless, he was not doing well and was completely poor. He often stayed in homeless shelters.

Then came the "Great War," "The War to End All Wars."

Hitler enlisted, and he did very well in the German army. He was decorated for bravery and made the rank of corporal. Rank was hard to attain in their system, it was very strict. But Hitler adapted. He was obviously motivated. He received the Iron Cross, and the German equivalent of a Purple Heart. It was the only place he had

---

[1] People may quibble about the historical facts. I think the broad strokes are accurate. This is not a history book, and details of historical events are irrelevant to my point in writing this.

ever succeeded. But the war ended in defeat. He was embittered and thought the German army had been betrayed.

In reality, it was a stupid war, one that should never have happened. It was really about three aging empires, the Ottoman, the Austro-Hungarian, and the Russian. It was about a system based on inherited titles and ancient conquests. It was about loyalties arising from the family relations of so-called aristocrats, the descendants of murderers and pillagers. It was about the dreams of empires, supported in lavish lifestyles by the sweat of conquered indigenous people far away. It was about feckless men arranging interlocking treaties with one another that did nothing to serve the people they were too self-absorbed to lead. Thus, one Serbian rebel shot an Austrian Duke and millions of human beings perished in an ocean of blood and sin. It was horrific and, I believe, indefensible. We live in a world of sin and blood, and sometimes the sane have to defend themselves from the insane. But while taking nothing from the courage and sacrifice of the soldiers who fought, WWI was total insanity.

However, this does not negate in any way the fact that God is sovereign over all things. I do not suggest that I know the mind of God, or can speak for Him in any way. However, one possible explanation is that God used the horror of WWI to prepare the world for the even more horrific things that Satan was planning for the rest of the twentieth century, NAZI-ism, communism, etc. As terrible as all this was, I am certain God used it according to His purposes, and that in the long run, God's purposes will be revealed.

The "peace" that followed was also insanity. The placing of the entire burden on Germany of paying the winners for the cost of the war ensured economic collapse and suffering of the German people. The Weimar Republic, the government established as a puppet by the victors, was one of the most corrupt since the fall of Rome. Bad policies elsewhere resulted in a worldwide depression that hit Germany and other European countries hard. Germany suffered a monetary collapse, paving the way for evil to rise to power.

Throughout this period, evil was gaining strength in the world through the lie that man could, via his own efforts, create a utopia, a just world based on the concept of collectivism. Russia had actually gone over to communism in 1917, but collectivist "theology" was alive and well in Italy, Germany and Spain; and had adherents even in England, France and the US. It went by various names, socialism, communism, national socialism, fascism. What they all had in common was the idea of central planning and theoretical national ownership. In reality, all resulted in forced obedience to a central figure or power group, no less sinful and avaricious than the old aristocracy, and sometimes even more bloodthirsty. But the seductiveness was for those who believed that the old system was unfair; and that, at least in their new world, they would have as good a chance at achievement as the next person.

The entire thing was a lie, but there also was another lie gaining popularity simultaneously. It was the lie that the Jewish bankers were responsible for the war, and in fact were pulling the strings even as the post-war world fell apart. Building upon pre-existing antisemitism that was rampant in Europe, it also took root in the mind of Hitler.[2]

Although it turned out that he was a gifted speaker, it wasn't brilliant oratory that drew people to him; it was his passion. People could feel the anger in him. If you watch any of his speeches, even if you cannot understand a single word of German, you can see by his gestures and voice and tone that he passionately believes what he is saying. This was not some artifice created by clever coaches for a professional politician. This was heartfelt emotion. And people were drawn to it, because they also felt similar emotions. And it was the anger, the prideful, self-pitying kind of anger that the wronged justify themselves in feeling, that results in revenge and destruction and blood—that let the devil take hold of a continent. I stated that I think everyone has a little evil in him, that the devil just needs a place to gain a foothold and establish a beach head. I confess that I am not an exception, sadly.

There was a time when I used to frequently fantasize chopping my father up with an axe. I told you that I had harbored resentment toward him, that there was evil in my soul. My father brought out all

---

2   There is some historical debate over whether Hitler was already anti-Semitic before the war.

my anger, wounded my pride; he made me feel powerless. Sometimes I truly hated him. The unearned meanness, belittling humor and the earned punishments, all added up to a fear and hate that I felt toward him.

My father used to snore so loudly you could hear him all over the house. I lay in bed sometimes and imagined the whole thing. Catching him asleep, whack with my scout hatchet, the blood. It is a *horrible* memory to me; one I would rather not have, but I tell it in hopes that sharing these feelings will convince you of my sincerity, because no one would tell such a thing on himself if it were not the truth. Had I actually done such a terrible thing, and even if I had gone to prison, would Jesus have come to my cell to save me? You betcha.

I have met men who were saved in prison, even murderers, who met the Risen Christ, and were changed and became Christians. After being saved, were they every bit as welcome in the kingdom of God as you and I? *Emphatically, yes!* Jesus came to save sinners, since the righteous do not need saving (Luke 15:7). But unfortunately, we have *all* sinned and fallen short of the glory of God (Rom. 3:10–18).

So the "werewolf" was my childish way of dealing with the evil tendencies *I saw in myself.* I didn't even yet have the terminology of Christian thinking at the time I saw the movie. But I knew what it meant to be mean, angry, self-pitying, and selfish. We do not want to be the werewolf, but when we are bitten we all have the urge to bite back. And he who is bitten is doomed in the movies. And but for Christ's blood, sinners like me would be condemned.

We should remember, Hitler didn't kill six million people by himself. There were Himmler and Goebbels and others. There were thousands, millions who participated in the slaughter in the Holocaust. Men who pushed old people, starving women, even children into gas ovens. *Were they also the antichrist?* Also, what about Stalin, Mao, Pol Pot, Saddam, Castro; the list could go on and on. Add in people nearby like John Wayne Gacey, Jeffrey Dahmer, and all the other mass murderers. And the cartels; "El Chapo" Guzman, who has had people beheaded by the dozens, and dissolved bodies in vats of chemicals? Add the anonymous man who just decides "for no reason" to kill his own family? Aren't they also just as evil? But it is not *their* evil I need to be concerned with!

Are we so completely different? If Hitler is burning in the lake of fire, and were I to go there because of my own evil, even though the whole world knows about Hitler, and very few know about me, would I then be different, or the same?

My concern is that the evil we have to be truly frightened of really is, for each of us, *our own evil, that dwells inside of us.* That place where Satan could get a foothold and start to tear down all that is good in us, and grow evil in its place like some maniacal parasite, until it kills the host, body and soul. I know, I have the potential for evil inside myself, and Satan knows it too. This is a war I have to fight, a battle for my life and soul that *I have to win with God's help.* For I cannot win on my own.

If you don't know about your own evil, I apologize for being the one telling you about it. Better to know and be ready, than to be caught unawares. At least you are not alone!

In my life, my personal experience, I always have to be on guard, because (1) sin is seductive; (2) evil often comes in with a friend or lover (who may not be a "bad person" from a worldly perspective); (3) evil, or temptation, comes when we are not ready; (4) I am vulnerable when I am sad, but also when I am happy; and (5) evil can hide itself in my pride. I constantly need God's help through the Holy Spirit to help me in this. Are you like me? See Romans 7:14–25. We all struggle with sin.

Therefore, *I forgive my father, and I recognize that there was good in him, and accept sole responsibility for my own evil deeds and lack of readiness when evil came to my soul.* I cannot excuse my evil, or any of my other evil acts, because of my childhood, or my parents, or anything else (Jer. 31:30). I have accepted the complete evilness of my own deeds, *sans* excuses. I am forever sorry for some things I did, and the people I hurt by them. I am blessed to know that Jesus will take care of our hurts, and God will wipe every tear from our eyes! (Rev. 7:14–17).

I believe that it is by accepting responsibility for, and owning, our own evil and our need for Yeshua (Jesus Christ), that we defeat Satan.

4. CAMP

I still, by fifth grade, had not adjusted to the new school. My teacher was a tyrant. I was bullied by some of the boys on the schoolyard. I was not doing my homework, and was regressing at times. My parents had noticed that I had been very rebellious at home, and I was failing academically. I was in trouble and being kept after school a lot. I was wearing them out as well.

Therefore, they made the sacrifice to send me to a YMCA summer camp. It was very inexpensive for what I received, but we had little extra money. This was a huge blessing for me, as it gave me a chance of socializing with other boys my own age who did not have a preconceived idea about who I was or should be. I also benefitted tremendously from the physical activity.

I remember the first time I went in the pool. I was ten, but had never learned to swim. I was unable to figure out how to breathe in the water, I was desperate for air. I nearly passed out before I realized I was in shallow water, and I just had to touch the bottom with my toes and stand up straight to breathe. I learned to swim after that and always enjoyed the water.

We not only learned to swim, we took hikes, learned about the woods, built campfires, and spent rainy days in a cabin with nine other boys. The hikes were hard for me, because I had no wind endurance. This was very beneficial, in that I started to gain the ability to do more prolonged physical activity with confidence. I was chubby and started losing a little weight.

Many of the camp councilors had been in the Army. We had revile and flag raising every day, taps at night. We had group meals and chores. We said grace. We sang songs. The Sunday outdoor church services were beautiful. The net result was that I grew in body, mind, and spirit.

I realized, after the summer at camp, that in order to have friends, you have to be a friend. I resolved to be more like a friend and to try to do better in school.

5. GROWING UP

I am not going to divert us unnecessarily by explicating all my teenage years. I had a small circle of friends. I was not particularly popular, and was never good at sports. I was lucky in that there were no drugs or pot in our school in the early sixties.

We did, however, have some vices. We all smoked. And we discovered alcohol in our early teen years. You were definitely uncool if you didn't.

My best friend and I got a quart of beer and chugged it in an alley. We could feel the effect, being unused to it. We liked the feeling. The world seemed brighter for a little while. Unfortunately, my friend eventually became an alcoholic and died early. It had long term effect on his life. I am sorry that this happened. We did not understand the risks we were taking.

On Friday nights, we had several of us that used to go cruising in my friend's '49 Dodge. We would get alcohol fairly easily in those days. Most of us didn't have girlfriends in high school. We weren't on the football team. I did go out once in eighth grade, over my parents' objections. I never really made the team, and only got in one play, the last game of the season. At least I tried.

My sister discovered a small Lutheran church that had an active youth program. We decided to attend there. The pastor was a younger guy and more hip than the one we were used to and his sermons did not center as much on hellfire and damnation. We liked it and joined. I hoped for a deep and abiding faith. I read the Bible. I went to prom with a girl there who was a year younger than me.

After graduation, I started community college. However, other influences were competing for my attention. I began to date girls and hang out with students. We liked to visit college bars. Some of them served at eighteen in those days. The music sometimes had a darker turn, and it always induced girls to want to dance.

The adults in church did not seem to be very inspiring I thought they were mostly no different from those at other places of worship. No interesting thoughts ever crossed their minds, I thought.

The Christians in the Bible were interesting, exciting people. They lived a dangerous life in dangerous times. Banned by the powers of Rome, pursued, their leader executed, yet they grew and blossomed and changed the world. Christians of the sixties sat in church, went to their jobs, and never did anything interesting. They were predictable. One fellow, lecturing me, told me our city was the "machine tool capital of the world." Yawn.

Of course, what didn't dawn on me, was that some of these same fellows twenty years before had stormed the beaches in WWII.

Church, I thought, was a place, a building. People recited prayers they didn't compose, and sang songs their ancestors had sung. On Sundays they usually sat in their same pew, next to their same friends and neighbors. They swallowed bread or wafers, wine or juice, and were forgiven their sins, if they had bothered to commit any. They were not bad people, just uninspiring and boring.

Again, this was the thinking of an eighteen-year-old, who, for all my life had felt like an outsider, never really a part of a community, or of a people, or even the country. Where exactly did I belong? Who were my people? Where were those who really accepted me?

At this same time there was a "new religion" starting in America. It came from the West Coast, where people, as we thought, wore almost no clothes and went surfing every day. Its "prophets" were Timothy Leary and Ken Kesey. We read about them and their promise of a higher spiritual reality. Their disciples were young, educated, attractive and enthusiastic.

They had much of Christian values woven into the fabric of this exotic belief. Peace, love thy neighbor, shun materialism, live and let live. "Dropping out" offered an experience of living, in some respects, like the original Christians, without the hang-ups and rules they preached in church buildings. Why wait till you're thirty and life's practically over? They promised a magic potion that would make you see God.

Of course, we were doing it all wrong. Salvation is not, and cannot, be found in a pill, a few drops of a chemical, or the flowers of a plant. In case you didn't get the picture from Adam and Eve in the Book of Genesis, the human race had already "been there, done that." Nor had anything changed since. Mankind had already acquired the knowledge of good and evil, and had not become gods, as the serpent had promised. The human condition was set down and man alone (i.e., without God) is powerless to change it. There are serpents and false prophets in every age to lead us astray. A whole generation attempted this, and it did not work.

I should mention that my father had passed away during the winter from a heart attack. It was a surreal experience. My mother had used his $1,200 life insurance as down payment on a little house. She and my sister lived there together and my sister went to college nearby. I had no tears. I thought I must be a bad person, for not mourning my father's passing. But it is something you just can't fake.

I married one of my fellow converts. For the next two years, we were the quintessential hippie couple. When it became apparent that the "new religion" was going nowhere, I was already looking for another. I tried Buddhism and yogic meditation. I became a vegetarian. My spouse was more into flesh. The religion fell away, and so did she.

6. MY TIME ON THE ROAD

My depression, at the time, was short lived. People were hitting the road that summer. All over the USA, kids were along the roadside hitchhiking. People were heading for parts unknown. It was a time of adventure and discovery. People who were college students, people who had decided to skip college altogether, guys who had been to the war and come home, eager to start living life after the military on their own terms. I was eager to experience similar things. The romantic notion of taking off for parts unknown was irresistible. I fancied myself being this romantic poet-philosopher, a vagabond and an adventurer.

I put into a backpack a change of clothing, an extra pair of socks, a light summer weight sleeping bag, a pound of brown rice, a bottle of vitamins, and two books, Siddhartha, by Herman Hesse and A Coney Island of the Mind, by Lawrence Ferlinghetti. A friend who had been in the army gave me his field jacket, which was barely worn, and a pair of heavy leather Army boots, perfect foot protection for the life on the road. I had $40 pinned inside the jacket for emergencies and a small folding knife that had been my father's. Thus equipped, I spent the summer on the road, a hippie vagabond and free spirit. I had a few narrow scrapes and close calls, but I emerged energized, suntanned and more self-confident than I had ever been. Then I met a girl.

Actually, it wouldn't be honest to leave it there. I woke up one morning on a park bench in Erie, PA, near the Greyhound station. I'd come in late from Buffalo, on the bus. I had been to the Canadian border, but the border guards weren't letting in young Americans without means. There were no more draft dodgers; that had been ended. They just didn't want us in Canada. They were afraid we might stay. Buffalo was just a mean town. Angry young men seemed to be everywhere. When I was waiting for a bus to the next town, a group of them were cruising the bus station. One of those had a .38 tucked into the front of his belt. That's the kind I mean.

Sitting on the bench an older man approached me. We talked. He said I looked like I could sleep. I told him yep, I could. I went with him to his efficiency across the street. He fixed breakfast, and we had some bacon and eggs. We lay on the bed for a short nap. Then we went to the liquor store across the street. He said I could leave my pack and coat while we got a drink. I bought a Dollar-fifty bottle of sweet wine and we were drinking it in an alley. There were three acquaintances of his also there. One of them threw up. I asked to go back up and get my stuff as it was late in the morning.

That is when I realized I'd been suckered. He said "I don't know what you talkin' about. I got some young white boys beat your ass." I needed to think fast. I went in and bought another bottle of the same elixir. I held it out to him and he followed. I led him all the way to his door with that, waving it in front of him. He followed as if entranced. After we got inside, I handed it over, grabbed my stuff, and headed out.

I hitchhiked out to Chicago, and on to Denver; then Boulder and into the mountains. I rode an inner tube down a fast mountain stream, saw an eagle flying from above. I read Siddhartha sitting alone by a mountain stream, and realized my birthday had passed unnoticed. I dove into a pristine lake up on the glacier with water temperature near freezing, and sunned myself on a rock in the middle to warm up.

I will never forget the night sky. I never appreciated how many stars there really are. The sky is so big when viewed from high up in the mountains. One night several other hippie travelers and I lay under the stars and just watched for a long time. The shooting stars were a light show. Dozens of them one after another. It was literally breathtaking.

Angry landowners eventually chased us all out of there. I caught a ride back to the Windy City with a group of college students from Wisconsin, and from there hitched to Lexington, stayed there a couple weeks, I went camping in Red River Gorge, with a friend. Then I hitched back up to Cleveland, to stay with friends.

It was after that that, reflecting on the memory of the people I had met, and in particular, in that alley behind the liquor store in Erie, PA, that I got a clear mental picture of street life. Those winos in that alley were me in ten years, maybe less, on the path I was going. It all seems so easy on the front end, but the fly gets caught in the honey and dies a very slow, painful death at the back end. The life on the road is romantic, but there is really no payoff, not for most people. Most people wind up alcoholics, beggars or in prison. Some wind up dead on the street and nobody knows who they were, or what happened to them. Nowadays they often just OD. Their life then is not romantic, or meaningful, or pretty. It's just over.

Then, I met the girl. We got on really well. Although I was on the rebound, she was someone I would have liked any time. She was someone you could talk to. I'm as attracted to pretty girls as anyone, but I could never really get on with someone that I couldn't hold a real conversation with. She was one that you could talk to all night. I never got tired of her. There was always something to say. We took an old car and toured the American Southwest for two months. We saw the Grand Canyon, stayed in Jerome, AZ, saw the Petrified Forest, redwoods, the Pacific Ocean, and many other things. We ate out of a cooler. I showed her how to make beans and cornbread over a campfire. We got poison ivy. By the time we returned we had decided to get married.

For a long time, my second marriage seemed perfect. We were in every way compatible. We had similar ideas, similar interests, the same friends, we were close emotionally and physically. For the most part we had a healthy lifestyle. Her father was a businessman. It was determined I should go back to school and get my business degree and she would finish nursing school. By this time I'd had so much college, it was easy for me. I even overcame my longstanding mental block with math. We both made straight "As." In my life, perfect things never last.

My wife began to experience bouts of depression. She sought help with doctors and psychologists and took medicines they prescribed. We stayed up long hours in the night talking, trying to solve this existential (as we thought then) problem. We thought if we could just figure it out, we'd be back on track.

Then, one evening when we were walking, she suggested we split up. It hit like a ton of bricks. I ran up the street twenty yards or so, grabbed my stomach and fell on the ground. Sorry, guess I was a baby. I couldn't take it.

We were living in a rented house. She took a one year lease on another apartment. The first night there was when I realized she was hallucinating. She saw people and things that did not exist. As far as I knew, she had never taken "hallucinogenic" drugs, and I had not either since my first marriage broke up. She, at some point was picked up by the police, wandering the street with her belongings in a shopping cart, even though she had paid a year's rent in advance on her apartment.

After that, her parents took her home to another city, and she was gone to me. Her father pointed out that she needed medical care. I found out her grandmother had died in an institution.

My resources were limited. I took a room near campus for thirty dollars a month. Days turned to weeks and weeks to months. Sometimes I talked to the family, but, I didn't have a phone, so it was limited. Several months later, she came back and took an apartment separately. We never got back together.

I will interject that writing these pages is excruciating. I feel guilt for not doing more to save the relationship, and for not knowing how to prevent, or fix, what went wrong with a person I loved. I am tortured by many of these memories. I have cried, I have screamed, I have gotten drunk and depressed, and wallowed in my misery. I used to sit in my $30 room and drink and listen to Hank Williams on the record player. My favorite was "I'm So Lonesome I Could Cry." Many a long, long night, feeling sorry for myself, I would listen to the tunes over and over, until, driven by despair, I'd go out and seek some company.

I joined up with a group of hippie potters. I made pottery on the wheel, which we sold at art fairs. I had a little money, but I had to stretch it out. Making pottery is meditative and it was a perfect distraction so I was able to think and heal. Firing kilns is very spiritual. Clay is soft, stoneware is hard. The heat from the kiln is so great you can actually get a "sunburn" at night. Earth and water and fire are very spiritual. But my more practical side told me I probably wasn't cut out to live and prosper this way.

I also made friends with the other guys in the rooming house. I took up a pagan lifestyle in a more serious way. I lived a few months in a group house with seven other hippie college students. It was during this time that I completely gave myself over to sin and the flesh and drunkenness, and anything else that "felt good" at the moment. Life was short, as I understood it, and pleasure was all there was in the end, wasn't it? I went where I wanted, did what I wanted, got high whenever I felt like it, and had multiple "girlfriends." I indulged all of my sinful desires as a way of life.

I know that God, despite my ignorance and profligacy, used all of this to bring me to the place I now am, and He uses my present pain in writing this to accomplish His goals. Had I not done the things I did, I would have nothing worth telling you now. And if you benefit from what I am going to say later in this writing, if it strengthens your faith even a little, then it is worthwhile. It is always worthwhile to suffer to help another person. It is, however, *not* a justification of sin to say, "*Shall we go on sinning so that grace may increase?*" Romans 6:1. Rather, I am simply telling this as an acknowledgement of God's supremacy over everything.

It was a crazy time, but I finished my degree in psychology. I was getting long in the tooth for the life I was living, and even for me it was getting old. It was nearly ten years since I graduated from high school, and where was I? Many of those I was hanging out with were several years younger than I. I didn't think about it that much at the time, but I was way behind and I would have a lot of catching up to do.

Some people might wonder if I really loved the women I married. I forgave my first over and over again, and I tried to make it work. Sometimes, things just are not under our control. I still forgive her, but I could never live with her because it hurt too much. So the answer is that yes, I know what love is, and my love has always been real. I guess some people would become self-protective and harden their hearts as a result of the slings and arrows of life, but I thank God I did not. I do not think this makes me better or worse than anyone. Am I needy? Maybe. I think, because of my experiences in life, I am able to make room in my heart for the addict, the drunk, the homeless person, the unwashed, the street people, and all the others that our society throws away.

7. "Grown Up" Life

It was after all this that I met the love of my life that I have been together with now for forty-four years. Unlike my previous relationship, we were not "perfectly compatible." But we shared on a very deep level. I think, looking back on it from my present perspective, it was partly because she had suffered. She was younger than I in years, but older in spirit. She had struggled with a disability all her life, had suffered a mother whose harsh treatment had made her life much harder, had had to help care for younger siblings, and had been shaken by the breakup of the nuclear family. She was, and is, a very bright girl, who was able to do the practical to take care of people, and who nevertheless loved literature and art and ideas. We used to read together, everything from Shakespeare to contemporary novels. We made each other laugh and had angry spats.

I had been planning to go to Arizona to graduate school in psychology, but chose to remain where I was and took a job as a nursing assistant instead. We were so different it was comical at times. On her birthday I (the romantic) had roses delivered. She (practical) said, "I thought I was going to get a Mr. Coffee!" It was delicious.

But sin does not just go away and the devil is crouching at the door. This is hard to write, but the habits I had formed the way I was living did not go away instantly either. Throughout the first few years of our marriage, I cheated, confessed, was forgiven, but it took a terrible toll. I am *miserable* recalling the look on her face when she asked what it was that she lacked, that others had. There was nothing. It was my sin that lived in me, that excused itself and belched forth. I don't like telling this, most of my friends don't even know it. I have to be honest.

And there was drunkenness. I'd gotten used to drinking a lot. I got so drunk that I threw up and pitched forward into my own vomit and passed out. I was jealous, uncouth, mean and awful. How it is that she stayed I don't know, but I do know and can swear that I loved her with all my heart. It makes me cry that I made her suffer even more after all she had been through. I am blessed by God to have gotten through those years still with her, to have raised our boys and that she is with me now. She's made of stronger stuff than I am. And our relationship is better than ever at this point.

There are many other things I could relate, but this story has a purpose and explaining or justifying my life and my actions is not that purpose. I put these anecdotes and experiences into the story to create context, so you will understand I was just a fallible person, another fallen member of the fallen human race. The fact is that I was a sinner, as is everyone else. Everyone has their own stories and experiences, all are unique. Some have not done anything like the things I have done, some have done far worse things. Many have done far more exciting things, fought in wars or explored uncharted lands, been astronauts. All of us were made by God for His purpose, and all of us are brothers and sisters, like it or not.

I'm reminded that we did nothing to deserve God's grace in sending His Son to shed His Blood for us. We deserved death, we deserved hell. We are sinning, weak, broken human beings, *"While we were still sinners, Christ died for us"* (Romans 5:8). I gave up most of my worst habits many years ago, though I remained haunted by some of the memories, but I committed all new sins.

I have believed through most of my adult life that I was a "good person." I tried to be "nice." I was kind to patients when I was a nurse, and most of the time to clients and other lawyers, when I was a lawyer. I was generous with friends, I loved my family. I gave to charity. Christ made the case in the Sermon on the Mount that even tax collectors and pagans do such things. See Matthew 5:43–48. These are things that are expected in human society. They are also things that other people reward us for with their approval. See Matthew 6:1–4. So we do not earn points with God by doing these things, as even pagans and sinners love their own families most of the time.

Skipping over many details of my life at this point, I worked various jobs. I went back to college to get a two year nursing degree. I worked in ICU, CCU, and Open Heart ICU. At one point, I was still unable to support a family in the way I wanted, to purchase a house, which I felt I had to have. I didn't want to raise my kids in roach-infested apartments. I just hated those places I had lived in all my life. (This was also in the era of double-digit mortgage rates.)

Therefore, I decided to go to law school. I took the LSAT test, and found out I could get a scholarship for tuition and books. It took three years to do that, but, I felt it would be worth it. The first semester, I aced my courses. By the middle of my second year, I was working as a law clerk for a small law firm.

I had spent my evenings in the back downstairs of the library studying after everyone else had gone, until the ten o'clock closing time most nights. Though I was on scholarship, I was forgoing my employment and I was not going to waste any opportunity. I finished in the top three in my class, and won many academic awards. I published an article in the law review.

I was equally dedicated as a lawyer. I worked nights, and almost every weekend for fifteen years, making partner in seven. This is not to brag, but just that you should know my personality. I was strongly of the opinion that people get what they deserve in life. This is certainly the ethic of our society. It is largely a myth. And thank God it is certainly not true in a spiritual sense.

After the bar exams, we decided to have a baby. My wife and I used to take walks around the neighborhood. She liked to show off her "baby bump." She glowed, and she was so beautiful. I loved the pregnant Mrs. *so much*! Our first child was a beautiful, healthy boy. He filled our lives with joy, laughing and wonder.

After our first child was born, we bought our first house, had a second boy. Our house was a beehive of activity. The next several years went by too fast. My wife painting and fixing, the growing boys and their friends running around and playing, laughing and shouting. We had vacations in Florida and Christmases and birthdays. The boys started school. Sadly, my mother passed away from a heart attack. She was seventy-nine.

As time went by, I advanced in the law firm and eventually became a partner. We moved to a nice house in an affluent area, with great schools. Our neighbors invited us to the church we eventually joined. We lived a very conventional life.

Problems, though, developed at my work. I tried to reach out to expand my practice and sought connections with some other attorneys. I had intended to expand into new areas and legal avenues. My firm invested in the project, but I believe everyone wasn't on the same page, and some people expected a payoff more rapidly than was realistic. I had given up other parts of my practice to devote myself more fully to the project. At a certain point, the firm broke up the deal, and I was "hung out to dry." I was unable to make my fee quota, and it would take too long to reestablish the practice I had had.

I went into a deep funk. I didn't know what to do. I had passed up numerous offers over the years, so that I could stay with the firm, but offers had all dried up when I needed them. I was over fifty years old and didn't think anyone would want me.

I was so depressed I was considering killing myself so the family could have my life insurance. I was actually planning to kill myself, and planning my family's finances. I didn't think about how the kids would feel, because I was so self-centered and messed up! I forgot to pay bills. My wife had to take a job to keep us going. I felt I couldn't face my partners. Obviously, I was not seeing God's hand at work in this time. I actually cried when I was alone. I prayed for God to help me. I felt I was close to the end.

But He must have been listening, because, the next day, He put the thought into my head to call a friend who worked at an insurance company, with whom I had worked on cases over the years. My friend asked if I had handled medical malpractice cases. I told him it was an area I had experience in, and sent him a resume. As it turned out, I was hired, and eventually overcame the problems I had been suffering with. The next few years I advanced in practice and in the company. I enjoyed the work and the people I worked with.

In 2010, I had a comfortable home in a suburban neighborhood, two late model cars, two teenage sons, and one hardworking wife who managed the home front. I did still work long hours, but had gone from a seven-days-a-week schedule with a small firm to five-days-a-week in a corporation. I had a long drive, but it was worth it. I had a comfortable six-figure income.

Of course, life is never perfect. From time to time, my wife and I had terrible fights. Most of the immediate arguments were small, but behind it were the fact that I had aged, put on weight, slowed down and was tired all the time. My back hurt. My wife was hard working, but she needed help with the house, the boys, the yard, etc. She felt abandoned and underappreciated. I felt tired and cranky. The fights were brutal, sinful, vulgar shouting matches in full sight and hearing of the boys. I am ashamed because, it probably affected their relationships for life. I think it is fair to say that I was prideful, and materialistic and we were both angry and unforgiving. I continued with work and family, church, and all until the next bump in the road.

8. PRIDE GOES
BEFORE A FALL

At the same time, we were becoming more accepted in the church we had started attending in 1999. Our neighbors had originally invited us to attend with them and soon after, we had joined. We regularly attended Sunday worship and we contributed with regular pledges. The church building is equipped with a German-built pipe organ that is the envy of the other churches in our area. We also had a professional organist and music director. The pastor was a gifted speaker. The Sunday services were impressive and the building is elegant.

In 2010, I was elected to be ordained an Elder and sit on Session, the ruling body of the church. We had a three-year term, a council of eighteen, with one-third being elected each year. We all also chaired various committees. The pastor attended and conducted meetings, but did not have a vote. Presbyterians are very democratic. Being on Session, many people were friendlier. I basked in the warm glow for a time. But there is always something that comes along when you do not expect it. Just as I was getting to be so comfortable, life happened.

The Saturday after I was installed as an Elder, we had a morning retreat, actually a first orientation for new Session members. The meeting ended at noon. As we were leaving, I began to have a pain in my back. It increased as I went to my car for the ten-minute drive home. Halfway there, as I neared our local hospital, the pain was escalating rapidly. I decided to stop. It was all I could do to give my car to a valet and go inside to the ER area. I threw up talking to a nurse from the pain. They got me into bed and gave me a shot and an IV, started collecting blood and urine samples.

The blood and urine were abnormal, with some blood in the urine and an elevated creatinine. They brought in a surgeon and by that time the pain was located in the right kidney area. They gave me a CAT scan to see if they could find a stone. However, there was no stone, so they discharged me with a diagnosis of "musculo-skeletal back pain." I was too out of it from pain medicine to really comprehend, but my wife was there by this time to take me. I had a prescription for Percocet.

9. A Brush with Death

Soon I was back at the ER. The medicine was not dealing with the pain at all. I was doubled over, barely able to stand. My wife was frightened and took me back. This time they put me on IV Dilaudid, a heavy duty narcotic pain medicine. On that medicine they had no choice but to admit me. Unfortunately, they did not recheck my blood or urine.

It was nearly midnight when the nurse asked me whether I had made urine since noon. I said no, I had not. When I was unable to go, someone gave me a catheter, and nothing came out but a few drops of blood. I was given extra fluid and Lasix, a medicine to stimulate the kidney. My labs showed a very elevated creatinine level, a sign of renal failure.

Then, Sunday morning, after a night drifting in and out, pain, medication, and a drugged kind of sleep, I was taken for an ultrasound test to look at the kidney. As the technicians slid the ultrasound device over the kidney area, one of them exclaimed, "Well, that's not normal." Of course, she wasn't supposed to say that. The other one shushed her. I asked what was wrong with me, she said your doctor is still doing tests and I'm sure he will tell you when he knows. I was starting to be upset. I said, "Maybe, if he was here he could figure it out!"

Upon arriving back on the floor, I demanded to see a doctor right away. The medicine had worn off and I was wide awake, in pain, but able to think. They eventually paged the hospitalist – a doctor who works in the hospital and covers a wide variety of situations when the admitting doctors are not around. He was a nice guy and I liked him. I told him my story from beginning to end, he looked over my chart. Next thing I knew, the room was a flurry of activity.

Three doctors appeared. They examined me and ordered more tests and blood work than I had ever had. Two of them I still see and one has become a good friend and mentor in Christian faith. (I have since wondered whether God had used this entire thing to bring us to know one another as a brother and sister in Christ. I have learned that He sometimes does things like that. But I do not know for certain. I can only testify to what I know.)

Eventually, after the testing and blood work, it was explained to me by a nervous young man who I assumed was a resident, that I had experienced a massive blood clot to the right renal artery, It was far too late to intervene, and the kidney was probably lost. Furthermore, it was likely that I would require hemodialysis and a renal diet. I figured I would be disabled if that came to pass.

The pastor from our church came to visit and pray for me, which helped my mood somewhat. I liked our pastor. They brought another man into the room in a bed opposite of the one I was in. He had had surgery and was in tremendous pain. I tried to encourage him and told him I was praying for him. It was obvious he was not getting enough medicine for the pain, and he was groaning continuously. I called the nurse and told her he was in too much pain. I felt bad for him.

After this they moved me into a private room. Maybe I was getting on their nerves, I don't know. I also had developed pneumonia, or fluid in the lung, and had to do exercises with an incentive spirometer. I was on massive drugs for pain, and was perhaps not fully rational. I thought I was going to die. Everything had this kind of sickening medicinal odor. It was somewhere between the smell of plastic and antiseptic iodine. It seemed to permeate everything.

I also had a consult with a dietician. I could not eat tomatoes, or oranges; and I had to use special preparation for potatoes, no restaurant potatoes. I had to forgo pizza, virtually all fast food, Italian food, all food that is high in sodium, and all food high in Vitamin K (green vegetables) because I was on Coumadin blood thinner. I asked what I could eat, and she said I could have white bread and hard candy. I was so upset, my wife asked her to leave me alone for a while. I wondered why they had not let me die. At that particular moment I felt I would have been happier.

I did not have the spiritual awareness to understand that what God was doing with me was for my good. I just felt it was all terribly unfair. I did not want to be in a hospital. I did not want to be on dialysis. I did not want to live on white bread and hard candy for the rest of my life.

The next week was extremely uncomfortable, even beyond the pain, which was constant. I would begin to sweat like I have never seen anyone sweat in my life. I would literally develop a pool of water in the bed. Hospital mattresses are covered with waterproof plastic so they can be fully sterilized. (I still had the catheter in, which handled the urine.) The nurses would check my temperature and it would be 102 or higher, and they would set about cooling me down. Then I froze and shook, and my teeth chattered so I thought they would break. It was the coldest I have ever felt. They would come in and put warm blankets on me and I would start to sweat again. This cycle was every two hours, twenty-four hours a day. The alternating sweats and chills continued for a long time after I was home, although it was much less severe.

Since the cause of the blood clot was not determined, I had to remain on the Coumadin for life. But I was blessed in that I did not require dialysis. The remaining kidney has regained function. For several years, the creatinine was elevated, but now it is almost normal. *Thanks be to God.*

The day my wife took me home I walked weakly out into the yard and kissed the ground I had thought I would never see again. Shamefully for a man, I wrapped my head with my arms and cried like a baby. The only other time I cried like that was when my mom died.

I was off work on disability for eight weeks. During that time, I tried to be useful writing coverage opinions for work. I enjoyed the quiet time researching and writing on the law. After my doctors cleared me, I returned to work, starting on a part time basis as I gradually regained my strength. My wonderful wife was so understanding and supportive, without her I don't know what would have become of me. She took me walking and we walked together, through the neighborhood as we have walked through life.

After I returned to work, it was exhausting. Not only work, but the long drive to and from, at least forty-five minutes each way, with heavy traffic most of the time, wore me out. However, I was able to resume my full load after a few months.

During all this time, I thought I would be lucky if I lived another five years and didn't require dialysis, which I viewed as synonymous with a kind of end of useful life. I prayed for a few more years, but my diagnosis of stage III renal failure seemed like a sentence or judgment. I determined to stick to the medical advice and hope for the best.

In any event, I decided to retire at sixty-six, three years after the blood clot. For those who have not reached that situation, it is emotionally and mentally draining. There are so many plans to make, so many arrangements to arrange. I had to hire an advisor to figure out the finances.

We decided that my wife should take a job for a while, which was a good financial decision. She had mostly been the homemaker, and the experience turned out to be good for her in many ways. She was able to find a steady job and keep it until she reached retirement. (She is slightly younger.) I think this experience was a growth opportunity for her, and she liked having her own income as well.

On the other hand, retiring and starting your own business at my age is possibly a little much, especially if you are not in your best state of health. I have tried to make a go of mediation as a part time business with not a great deal of success. Oh, I do the work well enough, but I am not much of a business man and I don't want to put the energy into it that it would require. I do enjoy it and like to keep up with people and with the law, but eventually, I will probably have to give it up. Everything in this world belongs at the foot of the cross.

The last day at work was tough. I packed my stuff in the car, and made rounds saying goodbyes. By the time I finished I had a lump in my throat and was holding back tears. It was so hard walking out of the building for the last time. I was leaving friends I had, the work I had done, the career I had built over nearly thirty years. Time to go home, all my diplomas and awards in a cardboard box to store in a closet. It felt like leaving my whole life behind. All the hours and days and weeks working, studying, poring over documents. All the moments that I had denied myself with my family. All the pleasures of living I had let pass by. And for what? A living surely. But there are other ways I might have had that. Now, instead, I have a box. It remains on a shelf in a closet to this day.

I had been an idealist, believing that this was the glue that holds society together. I was the Pharisee keeping the law, really. So much of Mosaic Law is in our law. Lying, cheating, and stealing. Reading Exodus chapters 21–23, you will see that they had a legal code very similar to ours. There were courts and lawyers in the time of Moses and in the time of Jesus. Paul chastises Christians for suing each other in pagan courts (1 Cor. 6:6). But idolatry, that is permitted in modern society. Not actually bowing to graven images so much, but worshiping ourselves and our "creations," like material possessions and money. Some would say it is encouraged.

To a great extent we have sold our legal system for a fast buck. That is why there are so many ads on TV for suing people. Had medicine? Sue the drug company. Had surgery? Sue. Worked at a job? It seems like whatever you might do in life there is always someone to sue. The jails and prisons are overcrowded. Crime flourishes. Money controls our politics. What is wrong with us? Could it be that we are just like the people two thousand years ago? Even farther back to the time of Isaiah? One has to wonder. Have we really progressed?

10. The First Day of the Rest of My Life

At least that was what I was looking forward to. I had set up to begin the mediation practice. I took a forty-hour mediation course at a local law school. I had a couple jobs lined up with friends to get that started. We had arranged for some work to be done on the house. I started painting our two-car garage that we used for everything except as a garage.

Of course, if you start a business and do not want to devote your life to it, it will not grow. But I still enjoy the mediations and it does keep me in touch with people and with the pursuit of the law, which I still care about.

I remained active in my church. I was on the finance committee. I attended services and gave money to the capital campaign, to remodel several parts of the building and put in a legal food service kitchen.

My wife and I also did several projects actually to update our house. A new kitchen and bathroom. Carpet in three rooms. I painted the house one whole summer. I had hobbies. We took vacations. I was a successful retiree with a comfortable income from savings and investments and Social Security. Life was good.

All in fact was good until a routine blood test revealed a PSA (prostate specific antigen) of 6.5. The doctor feared I had cancer and sent me to a urologist.

11. CANCER

The doctors are always calm and reassuring with a new cancer diagnosis. They tell you it is early, possibly benign even, small, all the usual things doctors say. The urologist decided however to biopsy the prostate. This now is a pretty easy thing done in a few minutes in the doctor's office. You are numb and it is done with a needle, but it does not hurt. I was able to walk out and drive home with simple discharge instructions on signs of bleeding and urinary blockage. I had a prescription for an antibiotic. The worst part for me is that I have to give myself Heparin shots before and after procedures for a few days to clear the Coumadin and restart it. That, and explaining to my wife that I might have cancer.

The biopsy revealed six of eight samples were positive with a "Gleason score" of seven. The Gleason scale tells the doctors how malignant the cancer is, and how likely it is to spread. The range is three to ten. Seven was considered an average score. I wanted to find the best treatment.

I have a hematologist/oncologist I have followed with since the blood clot. I had a follow-up appointment during this time period. As I told her about the cancer, she saw I was upset. She is a remarkable woman, who got her medical training paid for by serving in the Army. Obviously, I was under a lot of stress. I was concerned not just about the outcome of my illness, and having to make a possibly life or death decision, but also about the effect on my wife. I had planned also on having more time for us to be together after I retired and after she retired. We wanted to travel, walk on the beach; we thought we would have a long, happy retirement. So much for human plans!

Anyway, my doctor (knowing I was a churchgoer) spoke to me as no other doctor did. She redirected me to a higher plane, that God

48

uses our sufferings here to prepare us for His Kingdom. She didn't try to play down the cancer, she helped me see that God uses everything that happens for good. She gave me a long list of Bible readings and a copy of "Tramp for the Lord" by Corrie Ten Boom. Then both she and her assistant put their arms around me and prayed for me.

I walked out that day with a peace in my heart that I had not felt for a long time. They did not sugar coat the fact that I had a serious, potentially fatal, condition. Instead they redirected me to higher and greater things.

Neither one of them would allow themselves to be credited with any accolades for this. They would point out that *the Holy Spirit works through all of us to do all good things*, and, that is right. *God is the fount of every blessing.* We need to be careful not to puff ourselves up, and not to place other people on a pedestal. None of us can live up to being on a pedestal, for we are all sinners, reliant on the Grace of God. If you put anyone on a pedestal, you do as much harm to them as to yourself. I have apologized to my wife for previously putting her on the pedestal.

I honestly don't think (and this is just my opinion, as an ordinary person, not based on scripture) that God gives us cancer to teach us lessons. Just doesn't seem like the loving God I know. But it certainly seems possible that the devil might say "surely it's time to test this fat, lazy, self-righteous fellow a bit." The devil demanded to sift Peter like wheat (Luke 22:31), so there is a biblical basis for that part. And giving the devil his due, I was just a bit lazy, way too fat, *and* a bit self-righteous. Nor was I at all humble or self-sacrificing.

To be completely honest, I was scared inside. "No! Not now! I'm not ready!" But I was ripe for testing. God doesn't wait until we feel ready. He sees all, we do not. God uses all things, even calamities and floods and wars for ultimate good. Proud humans act as though we could see all ends, as though we could substitute our judgment for His. The truth is that I needed to have my butt kicked. In hindsight, this was a blessing, but it was a hard lesson to take.

We so often simply ignore, or try to just put it out of our minds, that this body of flesh dies. Human beings suffer. We experience loss and sorrow and fear and depression. Of course in this modern age the doctor has a pill for all of those feelings. We can continue to suppress them and deny reality until death comes calling. Then, you have to make some choices. You can numb yourself with drink or drugs, you can get "bitter and pissed off" (i.e., wallow in self-pity); or you can accept and face it. You can bow to the wisdom of the Creator, and try to do what He wants you to do with the time He gives. It seems to me (now, not then) that the last choice is best.

I had several consults to discuss options with the specialists. I saw a surgeon, two doctors who specialized in radiation therapy, and one whose specialty is chemotherapy. I opted for the Da Vinci robotic surgery. It is very advanced and the surgeon trained at Case Western Reserve, a top medical school.

The surgeon required me to have a series of imaging studies including an MRI with contrast, a bone scan and a CAT scan. There were spots on some of the bone images, but they were not conclusive, so we went ahead with the procedure. It was done in a brand new twenty-story dedicated cancer hospital. The operation was a breeze. I woke able to transfer myself to the bed from the stretcher. I walked the same night. I was still a little "high" from anesthesia, but I did not need pain medicine. I walked that night and went home the next day, with the catheter still in for the next week.

One week later, we saw the surgeon. The nurse took out the catheter, made sure I could empty my bladder and the surgeon came in. He busily explained the technical details. I asked, "Did you get it all?" His answer was "no." He stepped out for a moment, and I looked at my wife. Her chin was quivering. She is a person who doesn't get that look often. It was heartbreaking for me to see, that she was bitterly disappointed.

The bad news was that the margins were not "clean" and there were five positive lymph nodes. This meant the cancer was at least stage III. Very likely, it was stage IV. Stage IV, as I understand it, means that the cancer has disseminated to other parts of the body and surgery and radiation probably will not cure it, though they can buy time.

We opted to proceed with salvage radiation. This means, the area of the prostate and the places the cancer was found, the lymph nodes, and surrounding tissues would be radiated. I would have to be on special medication to knock out my normal hormone (testosterone) level before the radiation started and while the surgery healed. The hormone therapy prevents the cancer from growing, as it requires Testosterone to grow. This, however, is a temporary thing. After a period of time, usually two to three years, the cancer cells adapt and develop the ability to advance without it.

My wife and I had a long-planned trip to the West Coast, with reservations and hotel already booked, but we were concerned whether we could go with all the medical issues and the surgery. We decided to go ahead with our vacation. We knew there would be difficulties. I was still weak, and the surgery made me incontinent, so I had to pack supplies for that everywhere I went. Our decision was just to make the best of it in every way possible, forget the cancer, get out in the sun and see some things. It was definitely the right choice.

We stayed in a nice hotel in San Francisco, dined on Fisherman's Wharf, took Uber rides, visiting places like Land's End and all the galleries and quaint little diners and the fantastic mall in the Business District. We forgot budgets and just enjoyed ourselves.

We took the train up north and stayed with a wonderful friend, had dinner with several more friends, toured wine country. We took many pictures and made many memories. It was truly medicine for the soul to get away for this time and just be together. I had not spent enough time with just the two of us after the kids were born. My wife is a wonderful, imaginative, interesting person, whom I have loved almost from the moment we met in 1975. I had promised for years to spend more time with her, but life always got in the way. During the long train ride back to San Fran, I contemplated the time we had had together and the fact that I wanted to live the days of my life as precious one-of-a-kind days, aware of the limited supply. We had one more complete day in town, visiting galleries and dining at our favorite Thai restaurant across the street from our hotel. Then the long plane ride home.

I have always had a sad wistful feeling on the last days of vacations, a longing for the simple life, a wish to spend more of my time on the things I really care most about. In the end, the most beautiful and valuable things in this world are the people, especially the ones we cherish. Why couldn't we set things up so that we could spend a lot more time on the beach playing with our children, running in the sand, snuggled in bed with our beloved as the sun peeks through the curtains? Why must we endlessly pursue our careers and our things? Up at the crack of dawn, putting on our tie, grabbing our briefcase and heading out to fight the endless traffic jam and slurping down coffee at the traffic stops. Twenty-first-century life is custom made for the one who wants to tempt us to be angry, nervous, on edge, greedy, and all the other evil he dreams up.

When I got home, I had to take hormone shots in my abdomen and prepare for radiation treatment by having another set of scans. The surgery had been partially successful in removing most of the cancer, my PSA score was reduced from 6.5 to 0.5, but this meant there was still cancer somewhere, possibly bones. This cancer often takes up residence in bone, and there were spots on the bone scan that were suspicious. Actually the doctor doing radiation treatment was very cautious about the fact it might very well not be beneficial. However, she let me choose and I chose to proceed.

12. PROBLEMS WITH MY SOUL?

I spent the first few months contemplating life and death. Here is my problem. I *wanted* to be a "better Christian." I *wanted* unshakable faith, like Daniel in the lion's den. However, I wasn't really able to do it. I *tried* to do it with my mind. I tried to do it by "works." I tried to do it with my will.

The mind cannot, by wisdom, or by study, comprehend God's wisdom. God created everything in the Universe, known and unknown, including the human mind. He is the Author of the Heavens, and I am trying to duplicate him by my own human effort. I might as well be an ant.

> *"I will destroy the wisdom of the wise; The intelligence of the intelligent, I will frustrate."* (1 Cor. 1:19, quoting Isaiah 29:14)

Nor can good deeds ("works") possibly guarantee salvation. Salvation is given by grace, through faith. (Eph. 2:8)

Paul experienced "great sorrow and unceasing anguish" for the Jews of his day who rejected Christ. (Rom. 9:2) Although they sought after righteousness, they failed to achieve it, because they attempted to do so by works of the law (Rom. 9:32). Righteousness is given through God's grace (Rom. 10:3–4). The *only* path to salvation is by faith! Works will not avail.

> *See, I lay in Zion a stone that causes people to stumble and a rock that makes them fall; and the one who believes in him shall never be put to shame*
> Romans 9: 33

That stone is Jesus Christ, the Messiah.

The Pharisees of Jesus time strove to follow the letter of the Mosaic Law, in a theocracy run by human beings. Saul, who later became Paul (Paulus means small or humble) *was* a Pharisee. The Pharisees could not discern Jesus as the Messiah, though He fulfilled *every one* of the Old Testament prophesies about Him. They knew all the scriptures by rote, and could recite them verbatim, but could not see that standing right in front of them was the fulfillment of the very words they knew by heart! Nor could they by human reason explain why Jesus was able to do the miracles that He did. Still, they refused to believe the evidence of their own eyes. Nicodemus, another Pharisee, could not understand the meaning of being born from above, by the Spirit (John 3:10–12). Saul witnessed the stoning of Stephen (Acts 8:58.), who forgave even as he was being killed (Acts 8:60), but *still* Saul could not discern that he was a follower of True God. Later, when he was Paul, he regretted persecuting the people of the Way.

It is critical to understand therefore, that *I was tripped up by my own efforts.* I sat in the same church pew for nearly twenty years, said the same words, and *tried* as hard as I could to believe them all. I gave to the offering, to the charities, to capital campaigns, went to "work Saturdays," went to finance committee meetings, helped on the counting team after church services to count the collections. I considered myself a "good Christian." I was genuinely sorry for my sins, but was tortured by the memories of them.

Still, there was something missing. I had a spiritual illness that only drastic medicine could cure.

In the early twentieth century, syphilis was rampant in parts of Europe. It was considered incurable because Penicillin had not yet been discovered. Some tried the Arsenic cure. They used a carefully calculated dose of an arsenic compound, not enough (they hoped) to kill the person, but it made them terribly ill. Sometimes (for the survivors) it resulted in a cure, or at least a remission of symptoms. It was "kill or cure" medicine.

I have read accounts of how people, who were not raised in "Christian" cultures came to a deep faith upon first hearing the good news of Jesus Christ. In fact, the book of Acts is full of just such stories. People who have never seen, let alone read, the Christian Bible, come to a saving faith just by hearing the Gospel spoken for the first time! It is so *powerful*, it transforms them. What has happened to that power?

The Bible we know was assembled in the third century AD. The first printed version (not hand-copied) was not produced until the sixteenth century invention of the printing press, the Gutenberg Bible. The King James Bible, was produced in 1611. The chapter numbers we use to find references in the Bible were added in the thirteenth century, and verse numbers not until the 1500s. The Apostle Paul went to Greece and Macedonia with no books, although, as a Pharisee, he had to have memorized the Torah.

As he stated, Paul did not come to those lands speaking wise words, *lest the cross be emptied of its power* (1 Cor. 1:17). He came only with the Word of Jesus Christ, and Him crucified (1 Cor. 2:2). His message was counted as foolishness by the Greeks and nonsense by the Jews (1 Cor. 1:22). And yet, many believed, were saved and baptized and received the Holy Spirit! Why didn't I have the Holy Spirit?

Christ said it is as little children that people have to come to Him (Mt. 19:14). Little children hear and believe. God spoke to Abraham and Abraham answered, "*Here I am*" (Gen. 22:1). He had faith that God could do all things, and never doubted.

This kind of belief is much harder, I believe, for twenty-first century people, whether they were raised in church or not. Christian ideas and words are so much part of the culture that they have lost their power for many of us. We use the name of Almighty God casually, in vain. Even politicians invoke Him in political speeches having nothing at all to do with faith in Him. People even joke casually about Jesus, having no fear of God, and no shame because He died for us. Christian ideas and words are deeply imbedded in Western Civilization. But Christian ideas and words are not the same thing as Christianity. Real Christianity requires the believer to count the cost (Luke 15:25–33). Real Christianity requires us to love God and our neighbor (Mt. 22:37–40). *And* our enemies (Mt. 5:44).

So then, although I participated in church, and in my own mind tried to be Christian, there was much of the Bible I could not understand. For such a spiritual illness, I needed a harsh cure. *God sacrifices the flesh to save the spirit!* (John 6:63). Or as my wife likes to say, "You have to walk through fire."

Some people come in with childlike faith, and stay in the same mode for life. God bless them. But we are all eventually tested. Peter was "sifted like wheat" leading to his triple denial of Yeshua (Luke 22:31). Paul, The Apostle to the Gentiles, describes in detail the torture inflicted upon him (2 Cor. 24–33). He spent his final time in a cell chained to his guards in six-hour shifts and was beheaded in 65 AD. Peter was crucified upside down. We may never be called upon for this degree of sacrifice, but it is a fact of life that *everyone* suffers, and *everyone* dies the death of the flesh (Gen. 3:16–19). The issue, I think, is how we respond to that, either with faith, or by seeking our own path.

One more point I have to make. I have had friends, men who I thought were basically good (though we are all sinners), who committed suicide. These were people who attended and supported church and, I think, were like me. Like me in that they *tried* their best to believe, and *tried* to do the things the Bible says, as well as they could understand it. They listened to sermons preached by similar men, who *tried* their best in the calling God gave them. Yet they all lacked the *total faith that God had forgiven them, and was using their suffering to accomplish hidden purposes that we mortals do not see.*

This is so important; it needs to be the cornerstone of all spiritual teaching. They lacked the mature understanding that *whatever we suffer really is for His glory* and our spiritual wellbeing. They relied on human wisdom instead of trusting that "*For the foolishness of god is wiser than human wisdom*" (1 Cor. 1:25).

Jesus did not suffer and die so that we wouldn't have to. He suffered and died to give us a second chance. We still have to take up our crosses and follow. This is not just a metaphor. *We have to actually do it.* This means we have to sacrifice everything, sacrifice ourselves, we have to put others first. We need to be ready to give up everything.

I myself was nearly one of the statistics. I had considered suicide in a serious way. I had once been at the point of planning for the financial care of my family. They would have the money to live without me. I thought they would be better off. I could not see the damage such an act would do, because I was so preoccupied in my self-pity and fear of things I mostly imagined. I got through that time, by God's grace, but *the veil was still over my eyes.* The full truth of the Gospel as Paul preached it still did not get through to me. In fact, I had a hard time even reading the Epistles. They seemed opaque, and condemning. See 1 Corinthians 2:14. Reading Romans felt like condemnation, because I *was* condemned in my sins. I was drowning, I was unable to feel God's grace. I needed help.

The ones who killed themselves (and myself) were like the proverbial man, lost in a desert, unaware that there was water inches below his feet, if only he would drop to his knees and dig down a little in the soil. Somehow, the professional clergy and church welcome committee forgot to give us the roadmap to the kingdom when we came in the door.

13. MY FAITH JOURNEY

After finishing thirty-seven radiation treatments, I was processing all that had happened, and what it had meant, and how I could handle the changes in my life and the inevitability of death. Not that I had been ignorant of that, or had never really considered it. At one time I had been a nurse, had worked with many people who had passed, and the grieving families that often accompanied them, that cried and prayed and suffered with them.

I spent long hours in my chair by the window just thinking. I read the Bible a little every day. Much of it was hard to understand. I am a good reader, but the messages often seemed obscure, contradictory, and condemning.

This was what I prayed every night:

"God, thank you for this day. Thank you for all my days. Thank you for my wife and kids, our home, our life together, all our material things, our food, the times we've had together. I pray, if it be Your will, that this cancer be cured. Please be with our boys and with the people of the church and my wife. Bless our home and keep us safe. Amen."

Sometimes sitting in my chair took up the whole day. Sometimes I couldn't remember what I thought about, so from time to time I would pick up pen and paper and write something.

The year 2017 went by slowly. We took vacations, visited people, attended church, kept up the house. I returned to doing the mediation work, after recovering from surgery and radiation. On the cancer front, I remained on the hormonal treatment, so the PSA remained around the .04 level, the lowest, essentially, no active cancer. However, after my September appointment, the doctor wanted to stop it to see if I had been cured. In January, I would get the next test.

As the year 2017 drew to a close, my wife was preparing to retire her job at sixty-five, and it was as nerve-wracking as my own. All the arrangements, the financial plan, choice of health insurance, and all the things that have to be done to properly retire also caused her anxiety.

I came to two conclusions. I wanted to fight the cancer with all modern medicine has to offer and I resolved to get up and live every day God gave me as fully as possible. But how to do that? I have never been a particularly strong or brave person.

I have read about people who have done much harder things. People who are moved by the Holy Spirit. Like the Apostle Paul, they dare oppose the powers of this world even unto death. Like Daniel, they risk fire and death. Soldiers, twenty-somethings, who risk their lives in war every single day. People who ran *into* the Twin Towers on 9/11. People like Stephen, who forgave those who stoned him even as he was being killed. I wondered what it is that they had that I lacked. What kept them going even when they should have been frightened out of their wits?

When I was a kid we had a dentist in the fifties, who did not believe kids should have anesthetic. I know people who to this day will not go to the dentist unless it is absolutely an emergency, even though today's dentists do not let you suffer any pain.

Modern culture promises pain-free dentistry and surgery, and has a medication for every form of discomfort. Some pain is so bad even that doesn't work, but for the most part this is true. And we as a society swallow over the counter medicine by the truckload. We even have medications for emotions like grief and anxiety. Maybe that is why so many young people become thrill seekers. Maybe we have too much anesthetic and not enough of things that feel real to people.

Our ancestors tamed the wilderness, endured natural disasters with no one to come in on helicopters and save them. They were attacked by angry native people. No need to go looking for adventure in the Wild West, they lived it every day. Other than soldiers and first responders, most of us today never experience that. Most of the time, our lives by comparison are easy and safe.

The more serious problem for me however, was meaning. There were two possibilities. Either there were no God, in which case, why even go on, with pain and death inevitable; or there *is* a God, and all this *is* for a purpose. I was desperate for God to be more than a concept. But there is no proof. I wished there were proof. But *it was not proof I really needed. It was faith.* What I needed was the faith of Abraham; the faith of Daniel; the faith of Paul. Because, *we are all facing life and death every day*, just as much as they did, even if we are not conscious of that.

This is where I was with faith. Somewhere in between faith and doubt. Sometimes more faith, sometimes more doubt.

Thus I come full circle to the point of the story: Jesus. Why Jesus? Because in the end all roads lead to him. This is not some made up novel, *but real life and death.* Human beings really only have one choice in life: to take Him or not. *I am writing this for one purpose only, to bear witness for Him.* I would have been happy to not have to reveal all these things about my personal life. The Holy Spirit made me do it for both our sakes, yours and mine. I came home from church one evening, picked up pen and paper and wrote the first draft in forty-eight hours. I could not stop except to sleep and eat and take walks. My hand was having a hard time holding the pen. I wrote the first draft by hand in ink. I pray that whoever is supposed to take this to heart does so, that I will have borne fruit for His Kingdom.

Life is full of wrong turns and missed opportunities. If you have not yet surrendered to Him, read on. He is waiting for you, I am certain. All my pain will not be in vain.

As I said I have cancer, stage 4, and I do pray for a cure. As of now, they are doing treatment that buys time. There is a chance that immunotherapies will have a breakthrough while I still can benefit from it. That cure is not yet available. That means that if something else does not kill me first, in the next few years I will die of cancer.

Therefore I write in all seriousness and earnestness. There is no game, no fooling around. I do not care about money. Any profit that comes from this book I will give to the homeless people that I help care for.

I can see clearly now that we all live in the valley of the shadow of death from the moment of conception. Every minute, every day. We all whistle past the graveyard at night. *But we are also resting in God's gentle hands the whole time.* We are His children, and He cares for us. *Even when He sends us into the lion's den, he goes with us.*

14. Jesus

I finally come to the point of this entire story; Jesus. Yeshua. The Messiah.

First, I want to clarify a couple of things. I do not use drugs and have not for many years. I have never suffered from hallucinations. Not even when I did use drugs did I ever have a hallucination.

When I had these visions I was *fully awake and aware of my surroundings at all times.* I was not in any fugue or trance or altered state of consciousness. I was in my own home, alone.

I have testified to a number of witnesses about these things. I can assure you that if I did not believe them, I would not do so, nor would I write this. I am not crazy, have never been treated for mental illness, or claimed to have been abducted by aliens. This is just my experience as accurately as I can relate it.

In telling this, I am going to testify, telling it as fully and completely and accurately as I can. Obviously, this was a *vision* of the Lord, not Him in the flesh. He *will* return in the flesh, but not until the Day that is appointed, which no human knows.

It was a regular day, although the cancer was always in the back of my mind. I was in my house and had just gotten dressed as I was leaving from the back bedroom and headed down the hall. I had been thinking and praying and my thoughts were that I was trying to love others, but it was hard to love Jesus, as I didn't really know Him. I also felt that certain sins from my past were weighing me down, and it was my feeling I would have to carry them for the rest of this life, and hope I was forgiven in the end. I know these are mixed up thoughts. Suddenly, I was seeing one of my past sins in high definition, as clearly as being there in the flesh. It was every gory detail. Exactly as it had really happened.

I was still aware that I was walking to the kitchen. Then another vision of a past event. It was very real. I was holding the kitchen counter, as I saw a third vision of another past event. I was re-living all my past sins, and the thoughts and feelings that went with them. The things I had used as defenses were stripped away. Justifications, excuses, and rationalizations no longer protected me from the pain. *I was being forced to face the evil;* to face the full weight of the harm to other people. Some were from childhood, some from adulthood. I saw them one after another.

Lies I had told, infidelities, sexual sin, mistakes covered up, cruelties, drunken, profane behavior. Things I said that I regretted. *I was seeing every ugly thing I had ever done in my past.* With each one a weight was added to my shoulders and my heart. It was very much like those lead vests they have in the x-ray room at the hospital. Weight kept piling on me. I had to sit down. I got over to my chair by the picture window in the living room, just a few steps from the kitchen, and sat down. The visions didn't stop. The weight didn't stop getting heavier. It felt like I was being crushed. It was hard to breathe. I squeaked out "Jesus, help me."

That is when I saw His Face, slightly above and to the left of me, as I was sitting there. The voice said either, "I thought you were never going to ask" or "I thought you'd never ask." I am not certain which, they mean the same to me. The face appeared at first with emanations of red and yellow around it, as well as I can recall, just at the first. It was coming toward me.

I have the belief that appearance of the face I saw could be what I needed it to be. I do not know. However, so that you may believe I am telling the truth, and hiding nothing, it was a handsome face with a square jaw, and black beard and hair, dark eyes, big square teeth. It was a handsome, tan face.

Then I saw Him directly in front of me and slightly above me. He said, in a normal voice, "Do me a favor and toss that up here on this cross I'm carrying." I looked down and my sins were in a brown cloth bag, or burlap. I now easily lifted them onto the cross. It was a large oversize wooden cross. He said "I'll carry them with me up to Calvary." I saw other things up there also, like the weight of the world. I thought it must be terribly heavy. I think He knew my thoughts. He turned to me and grinned, a regular full grin. Like "Yeah, I got this." And he was gone.

But he came back one last time in front of my face, and said "after all, it's what I died to do." And once more, He was gone, taking my great weight with him.

The first thing I noticed was that the weight of sin I had carried, some of it forty, fifty, and sixty years was gone. And it has never come back in the twenty months or so since, as of this writing. I can breathe. I am not weighed down by the past, by my baggage, by sin, none of it. It was taken and put to death on the cross, washed clean by the blood of Christ.

I do not worry about the cancer, about death, about suffering. In a way, I feel it is a privilege to suffer and die for the One who suffered and died for me. As I said, I am neither brave nor strong.

Then one more thing happened.

The Spirit led me to pick up my Bible and took me to a verse I had read many times, but like a man with a veil over his eyes, I had read it without comprehension. It is sandwiched in between miracles like walking on water and feeding five thousand people with three loaves and two small fishes.

> *"Very truly I tell you, whoever hears my words and believes him who sent me has eternal life and will not be judged but has crossed over from death to life."* (John 5:24, NIV)

Here is how the spirit showed me to read:
WHOEVER! (including me!)
"Hears my words…"
"And believes him who sent me…" (Yes, I believe because of what I saw.)
"HAS eternal life…" (i.e., RIGHT NOW, present tense)
"And will NOT be judged…" (future tense, do not be afraid, you are ok)
But HAS crossed over from death to life! (past tense, it is done).

Past, present, future…the trinity of time!

Here is part of why this is so important: first, it does not matter WHY I believed. The fact is THAT I believed in Him. And because I believed, I have eternal life. The Greek word used, I looked this up, also means spirit life, as well as eternal life. I was dead, and like the Prodigal Son; now I am alive! It was done by the power of Jesus Christ, because I was truly *repentant*, sorry for the past, and honestly intending never to do any of those things again; because I *asked*; and because I *believe* in Him, who I saw in the vision.

I know that what I saw was truth, because when I saw those sins, every one of them was true, *exactly* as it happened. They were far more realistic and awful than ordinary memories. I know everything I saw of Christ was right, *because the admission of guilt and conviction of sin preceded it,*[3] and because everything is consistent with the Bible. I was fully awake and aware of my surroundings, so I know it was a vision, not a trance or stupor. I was wide awake, so I know it was not a dream. And it was *effective*, because the weight has not returned, though writing parts of this story have revived some unpleasant memories.

> *"For I will forgive their wickedness and I will remember their sins no more."* (Jer. 31:34)

Psalm 107:19 says:

> *"Then they cried out to the Lord in their trouble, and he saved them from their distress."* (NIV)

I had been in trouble, I was dead in my sins, when, without warning, cancer came to call. Church gave me some comfort, but I knew something was lacking. I *tried as hard as I could.* I attended Sunday worship, I read the Bible, I listened to the sermons, I took communion; I said the words. Still, what I needed was *transformation*. And transformation cannot come through human effort or

---

[3] Convicted, but not condemned!

intelligence, study or wisdom. The change in my life only occurred through the intervention of Jesus Christ, and the Holy Spirit.

This experience has changed my life. I am no longer weighed down by the past. I have been freed and I can serve the Lord in any way He wants without worrying. Cancer is ever present, *but I accept the fact that the death of the flesh is inevitable, and life of the spirit is assured.* If the Lord is with me, who can be against me? Of whom shall I be afraid? (Ps. 27:1–2).

15. THE PRIEST

I had thought this was finished, but there is one more point I am compelled to make. I pray with all my heart that my friends who are saved through their own respective churches do not take this wrong. As I have pointed out, I think those who take Yeshua in their hearts and believe in Him are saved, regardless how or why they got there. See John 6:40. And I think if it worked for you, Christian organizations of all kinds are fine and good. God is not prejudiced.

In my vision, Yeshua (Jesus) fulfilled the role of priest-confessor. This IS biblical (Heb. 4:14–16). Christ is THE Priest-confessor. He did not appoint Himself, but was appointed by God Most High (Heb. 5:5–6). *"A priest forever according to the Order of Melchizedek"* (Heb. 7:17).

Melchizedek first appears in Genesis 14:17–20. After Abram (who later became Abraham) rescues Lot, his nephew from invaders, he enters the Valley of Kings (Gen. 14:17).

> *Then Melchizedek king of Salem brought out bread*
> *and wine. He was priest of God Most High, and he*
> *blessed Abram, saying,*
> *"Blessed be Abram by God Most High,*
> *Creator of heaven and earth.*
> *And praise be to God Most High,*
> *Who delivered your enemies into your hand."*
> *Then Abram gave him a tenth of everything.*

There are some really interesting things about this. First, there was no established earthly priesthood until God gave the law to Moses *five hundred years after Abraham died!* Paul (or the author of Hebrews) said his name means "king of righteousness" and "King of Salem" means "King of Peace" in Hebrew (Heb. 7:20–21). The worldly priests under the law had to be descendants of Aaron, and to have a proven genealogy, but Melchizedek had neither, nor birth, nor death (Heb. 7:3). The author of Hebrews also points out we only tithe to one greater than ourselves, yet the Patriarch of the Hebrew Nation tithed to Melchizedek. Thus, Melchizedek was not an ordinary earthly priest, nor an ordinary worldly king, but a Heavenly priest, priest of God Most High! And Yeshua was appointed priest by God, after the order of Melchizedek.

The purpose of a priest is to intercede for us with God. The priest used to enter the holy place and sprinkle the blood of an animal to *cover* the sins of the people. But it is impossible for the blood of bulls and goats to *take away sins* (Heb. 10:4). However, Christ did not enter the holy place by the blood of animals, but by His own blood, perfect and untainted by sin (Heb. 9:12). His blood was sufficient and He sits at the right hand of God. *"For by one sacrifice he has made perfect forever those who are being made holy."* (Heb. 10:14). And God said, *"I will remember their sins and their lawless acts no more"* (Heb. 10:17, quoting Jer. 31:33) Then he adds: "their sins and lawless acts I will remember no more." (Heb. 10:17).

Furthermore, earthly priests are human and all humans still sin, even the saved. Therefore, they were only permitted to enter the Holy of Holies, where the Ark of the Covenant rested, *once a year on the Day of Atonement*, and they had to sacrifice a bull for their own sins, and those of the people. They entered the Holy of Holies by the blood of bulls and rams.

But Christ, who is perfect and eternal, entered God's throne room in Heaven, *by His own blood*. Since He intercedes for us at all times, no worldly priest is necessary. Yeshua is directly accessible to us, not only on festival days or on Yom Kippur, but continuously. He is accessible, not just in a tent made by human hands, but in every place to which we might go, even in prison or anywhere we might be in need of Him. We do not need to carry out any "works" to reach Him, recite any incantations or rituals. All I had to do was to call out to him, in my desperation, in sincerity and in my despair, "Jesus, help me." He heard my confession; He granted my absolution. I am eternally grateful to Him.

16. AFTERMATH

Immediately after this experience, I could not wait to tell someone; anyone. I could not wait to share the joy I felt at that time. I wanted to yell out, "I saw the Lord Jesus and He saved me from my sins." I knew I could run into a lot of pushback. I had never heard of *anyone* in my church in the twenty years I had been there, tell of any sort of dramatic salvation experience. When I was in my early time on the Session of my church, I once started talking about my personal gratitude and the fact I was amazed to be there, and I may have been a little bit teary-eyed, when I looked over and a couple of ladies were looking, jaws dropped, like I had two heads. We were there for business, not revelation, confession or the like. And certainly not tears. Awkward moment.

There was a very well-known local attorney once who swore he had seen Christ in the courthouse. He had had a radio guest spot on a popular station. He was publicly pilloried and humiliated. How do they (his persecutors) know whether he did in fact see Jesus, or not? And why did they react so negatively to what he revealed? He was ridiculed on the radio program where he had previously been a guest. Lawyers still joke about him, years after he passed, because he told the experience. Apparently, the devil didn't like it, and good people are recruited often to do his work.

> *"Blessed are you when people insult you, persecute you, and falsely say all kinds of evil against you because of me."* (Mat. 5:11, NIV)

Worse, many people would think I made the whole thing up just to get attention. *Not that I want attention.* It is the last thing I want. I would have been happy to skip writing my story altogether, especially the personal, sinful parts. I'm sure if certain people get wind of that, they will be clucking like a bunch of hens. Those who are supportive, however, will probably keep their mouths shut.

What else could I do? I could try to convince myself it wasn't real, like Scrooge, who after being visited by the ghost of Marley, laid it up to indigestion. But then, I would have been back drowning in guilt, sin, agony of the spirit. I would be the man who, on his death bed, looked Salvation in the eye and said "no, thank you." The full weight of all my worldly transgressions would be back. It was so horrible, perish the thought!

I had a redacted version I told people. Here is my Facebook post, typos and all:

> "I thought i was dying and i thought about my sins. i remembered all my lifetime, including things that happened as a child. Things i had forgotten. I saw them all with clarity. Too many. The weight was more than i could bear. I was crushed. I cried to the Lord, because all hope was gone. I begged Him to take the weight off me. To my everlasting amazement, i found He had been waiting on me. All I had to do was ask! I laid my burden on the Cross and He carried it up to Calvary. I have not felt that weight since that day.
>
> "Some people think I made this up, but its all true. Id be embarrassed to put it on here if I didn't believe it."

I gave a similar oral version to a few people. I had some who were nice, some who simply informed me that they "weren't religious." Of course, religion had nothing to do with it, but when the truth is set out and people reject it that is their free choice. I was not discouraged. I told my wife. As might be expected she said "what are your sins?" (She knows my sins against her, but it's a normal question.)

Being a saved Christian is one thing, living like one is another. I had a hunger for knowledge and guidance. I knew that the Epistles of Paul were supposed to be a guide to this area. I had always had trouble with this part of the Bible. The words sounded like condemnation, because I *was* condemned. They sounded impossible, because they are impossible without the Holy Spirit. But now I was not condemned. Now I was guided by the Holy Spirit. Now, the words made sense. My copies are worn. The pages are yellow with highlighter, and the margins are written and scribbled in. The pages are worn thin. They are dog-eared. I said copies. I use several. I like modern English because it's easier to understand, but I use NIV, NRSV, and other translations. I have not found any important differences.

Now, when Paul states we have all sinned and fallen short of the glory of God, I can read it without a knot in the pit of my stomach. The lake of fire in Revelation does not frighten me. I understand that we are all under the law of sin and death, until we are saved and given the Holy Spirit; saved by Grace through faith. Saved, though we were powerless to save ourselves. Saved by grace where works could not avail us. Saved by the blood of Christ, the only perfectly pure and untainted blood.

I was able to comprehend that the law and the prophets are summed up in two commandments, to love God completely, body and soul, and to love one's neighbor as oneself. Paul describes the kind of love he means. Love is patient. Love is kind. Love forgives. Love never leads another to sin. See 1 Corinthians chapter 13.

Love for a Christian is a spiritual love. The Christian spirit is connected to the True Vine. Every Christian is a member of Christ, like an arm or a leg is a member of the body (Rom. 12:4–8). This is why the Apostles, including Paul, were so specific about not allowing sexual immorality. Actually, love and sex are quite different things (Rom. 13:13–14). The devil likes to get us to confuse them. The devil wants to confuse us all the time. Why? Because he knows that clear vision and clear thinking lead to God, by necessity, since God created us and everything around us. Anything that blurs that vision is sin.

The cost must be reckoned by the newly saved person (Luke 14:25–27). This is that the body of sin must be put to death, first by baptism (Rom. 6:3–4). And then, ultimately, in the physical death of the mortal (fleshly) body. When you are baptized, you are joined with Jesus in his death (Rom. 6:4). You put sin and flesh to death and raise up a new creation in Christ. The *old you is dead;* the new you is *alive in Christ* (Rom. 6:11). *This is being born again of water and the Spirit* (Jn. 3:5). The process is not complete, however, until physical death takes the husk of the flesh, and it is cast back to the earth and subjected to corruption, and becomes the dirt from which it was taken (Gen. 3:19, 1 Cor. 15:42–43).

In my home church group, I felt strongly that the Holy Spirit wanted me to be baptized. This seems strange, since "I" had been baptized in church, by a clergyman putting water on my head and asking me the familiar questions. However, many of us believe that upon being saved, *we are really, literally, new creations in Christ,* because *we are born again.* I felt strongly that, since I had experienced a transforming salvation, with a vision of our Risen Lord, that I am now a new creation in Christ! Therefore, I was immersed in a pool and openly repented before God and man, *I submitted myself, body and soul to Him.* I said with my lips that Yeshua (Jesus) is lord, and believe in my heart that God raised Him from the dead. See Romans 10:9.

Everything we have in the end gets laid at the foot of the cross (some say laid on the altar; to me, same thing), the fleshly body included. Some people like to avoid this fact. But they are just putting off dealing with the inevitable reality they know they will have to deal with someday. Why stick one's head in the sand?

There will someday be a miraculous transport of the remaining living Christians to Heaven, and you might be here for that. But what if, just like everyone you knew who has already passed you have to die the death of the flesh? *I know I wasn't ready.*

Therefore, why not be ready? The fact is there could be an eighteen-wheeler or cancer or anything out there with your name on it. Nobody is ever completely ready for it when it happens. We are hit like a lightning bolt out of the blue. Sometimes, we never even see it coming. I think we should make ourselves as ready as we can mentally and spiritually. It starts with *surrender* to God's will. We know, at least me, I am not strong. I know I am not brave; I know I have little grace.

But Jesus Christ is strong, brave and full of grace. I ask Him to lend me some of those qualities from His vast store in my hour of testing. I am ever so humbled by the stories of martyrs around the world, people who suffer torture and die rather than renounce Christ. People inherently no different from you or I, but whom God's grace fills and the Holy Spirit inhabits for a day, a period of days, or for years. On average ten people every day die for Christ this way, in the persecuted countries.

But we have to prepare ourselves. We should pray to be more like them, to be prepared for whatever sacrifice God requires, and asking for grace and courage to meet that eventuality. Then the Holy Spirit will have something to work with. This is just my personal opinion, not something God spoke to me.

And being ready is not just ready for sacrifice or hardship. It is also for opportunities to serve, and opportunities to share in spirit. These will pass us by if we are not ready.

17. LOVE THY NEIGHBOR

I believe we are all called to serve Christ in different ways and we are all equipped by the Holy Spirit to do what God wants us to do. We are called at different hours. See Matthew 20:1–16, and to different tasks. We are given talents, each according to God's plan, and our needs, so that we are able to do what God plans for us to do. See Romans 12:3–8.

This is not a question of salvation being earned by works. Salvation is by faith, not by works (Rom. 3:21–26). But the Spirit calls us and we must obey. Like Abraham, when God assigns our duty, it is for us to respond, not resist.

We do the Lord's bidding *because we love him,* and we serve the poor because He asked that of us (Mat. 25:40). I felt called to serve the poor, *especially those outcast* and *held in low esteem by the world.*

> *"But God chose the foolish things of the world to shame the wise; God chose the weak things of the world to shame the strong. God chose the lowly things and the despised things-and the things that are not-to nullify the things that are so that no one may boast before God."* (1 Cor. 1:27–29)

Our society, the whole world, *throws away* human beings. It is a horrible, sinful fact. We abort babies, even up to the moment of birth. We neglect the homeless. NIMBYs refuse to allow rezoning, so that shelters for human beings can exist in "their neighborhoods." I guess they never got the part about "love thy neighbor." Some of our cities have thousands, or tens of thousands, of people living right in the street. There are tent cities, with medieval plagues spreading.

Eventually they will spread to everyone. Rats, lice, fleas and bedbugs proliferate and spread disease. One expert said that if the plague were to return, Los Angeles would be "ground zero," because there are now so many rats living in piles of trash, garbage and human waste.

So God calls us all, and *He called me* to do what I can to help whom I can in this world where sin is so dominant. We are all different in our gifts (see 1 Corinthians 12:7–31), and I pray God will use our differences for His purposes! I like to think that, in my life, He is doing so right now. (I will tell you that thinking about that fills me with joy and gratitude. I also pray that writing this is fulfilling His calling as well.)

God chose the homeless as my *first* calling of the spirit. He put it in my heart not to write a check, but to go to them *in person*. He put it in my heart to dress like them and go to them *humbly*, to work as a volunteer in the shelters. He put it in my heart not to tell anyone I was a lawyer, or to assume any status at all. To talk to them, to help hand out donated items, to do laundry, to mop the floor and set up chairs, to do whatever needed doing, so as to be a friend to them. When we listen to the Spirit, *we do everything for God's glory*, because it is not us that do it, but the Spirit of the Lord working through us that does it.

I inquired of various places, "Where can I serve?" Many had requirements, waiting lists. One did not. It is a "low barrier" facility, meaning if a person is intoxicated or otherwise impaired, he or she can still come in, provided they cannot bring any contraband in (booze, drugs, weapons); and they must behave while they are on the premises. Local groups or churches sign up to bring dinner, and we distribute donated clothing from the community. That was the job I liked best, because it gives me a chance to interact with the people. I don't mind when they are demanding or complain. I know it isn't personal.

The shelter is very crowded in the winter. There are seventy-five beds. It gets cold here in the winter. Shower and laundry facilities are limited. There are three restrooms and one shower. There is one clothes washer and dryer. A guest can only get clean every two or three days. On most nights, it gets below thirty-two, and at nine they can let in an extra twenty people who will sleep on mats on the floor. On the very coldest days, when it is zero or below, they let people stay inside during the day. On other days many of the people head to the public library. Some of the people there also have jobs, but in winter, there are a lot of more chronic homeless people, that have nowhere to go. Some have severe drug and alcohol problems and some are mentally ill. Some are just old and physically disabled. Believe it or not, there are also some people who refuse to come inside even in the dead of winter. There are people who are in and out of jail for minor offenses and a few who have been in prison and are trying to transition. Most of the beds are male, but, there are also some women. Nationally, I was told 80 percent of homeless are men.

I found that I love working with these people. As always, God knew exactly what He was doing. I was a little nervous at first, but after a year, I am very comfortable. Not that my comfort is essential to be doing God's will.

Most are grateful for what they receive. Obviously there are occasional behavior problems. A few manage to sneak in those little one-shot liquor bottles. Bags are checked, but the staff cannot do a thorough search on every person. If they are caught with contraband, they are given the night off. It is not done lightly, because on the street in the cold, they are at risk. A few are put on the list to not be readmitted. The paid staff do deal with most of the behavior problems, but I have broken up a couple fights. The worst offenders get to go out with the police, and spend a night in jail. At least they are safe. Mostly, I set up the dining room, make coffee, organize the clothing, hand out clothing, do laundry sometimes, and occasionally make beds. I have found that I enjoy those tasks as well.

But what I love is interacting with people. I talk to them, joke with them, occasionally talk about serious things. If they are receptive, I talk about Jesus, and tell them they can always go to Him. Of course, in this setting I can only do this if the individual is receptive. I try to plant little seeds and hope they grow. At first, I was too pushy, a couple guys may have been turned off. You have to learn.

Their lives are difficult. Outside it is cold and food is hard to get. Inside there are problems of a crowded facility and once they are in for the night they can't leave and return.

Life on the street is hard. A person has to be vigilant. They are all vulnerable. This is especially true for women and the elderly and disabled, the mentally ill, the addict. The drug supply on the street for the addict is all tainted with Fentanyl and other dangerous things now. Any drug purchased on the street these days is very dangerous. This includes pills, pot, powder, or whatever it might be. With some of them, the first dose can kill a person. Thus, the work of the shelter is life-saving.

One thing I like especially about this shelter, I did not have to fill out any personal information. After a year, they don't know I have a college education or that I am a lawyer. I am fairly anonymous. I am just an old guy that shows up to help.

The homeless struggle with anxiety and low self-esteem. The world looks at them with disdain, but we know God chose the things that are not to shame the things that are, and to nullify them (1 Cor. 1:28–9).

So all winter from November through March, I worked as much as I was physically able there. I am trying to get in better shape. We cannot labor in the vineyard if we do not try our best. My calling involves physical work, so I'm in training. I also have to get my shots. With the close quarters, you catch everything. You need to be immunized for flu, pneumonia, and Hepatitis A at least. I had a cold all winter last time. The guests fared much worse, with some nearly succumbing to pneumonia.

I tell you the truth, I got back tenfold for all I did. There were blessings from people and from God all the time. People knew me and greeted me by name, they waved when I pulled my car in. I was never lonely, never depressed, never worried about the cancer. I felt like I was "on a mission from God."

This summer, I have volunteered in the evening in the summer program. There is not much work, but there are needy guests. What they need sometimes is someone who will not judge or look down on them to talk to. Someone on their own level. So I listen and share with them, and for those who are receptive, we talk about the Lord.

Some are in recovery from alcoholism and addiction, some have been in jail or prison; some have been saved through the twelve step program. The idea of the summer program is to help the men get from homelessness to self-sufficiency. These men want a hand UP, not just a handout. It is a smaller number and there is time to get to know people and relate.

There are some amazing people. But they have had things go wrong in their lives. I am blessed by God to be able to do this. Even writing this book, I get down on myself because of things I did, because I am unworthy, because I am not a theologian or a writer. But after being with my people, sometimes having the Holy Spirit work through me to achieve a purpose or help a person in trouble, I am renewed in spirit and boosted in my heart. I was near tears driving home last night, after I held a father's hand and prayed for his son. *I wish I could bottle that feeling and hand it out to you.*

18. OTHER BLESSINGS

Two other blessings I had that made life terrific in this time were my wife and my new home church. My wife is a very strong and incredibly patient woman, who has been by my side through every trial and much more for forty-four years. She retired from her job almost two years ago, and we have been so fortunate to get to travel and spend wonderful time together. We take long walks holding hands. She is so beautiful, and such a blessing! We sit in the morning and drink coffee and discuss our day. I have described her as the light of my life, but that belongs to the Lord. She is however, my love, my sweetheart and my help in this world.

I have found a wonderful experience in home church. If you are not familiar with the home church movement, there are some of us who feel that institutional churches have not well suited *our* needs in spiritual growth, or even have moved away from biblical teaching in their program or doctrines. While I feel that these institutions play a valuable role, and for the most part do follow the Bible, I am personally disturbed by the preoccupation with issues like divestment from Israel, climate change, and human-conceived ideas of "social justice" that existed in mine. None of these are biblical. God set forth His righteousness in the Bible, and man *cannot* improve upon it!

I had attended the same church for twenty years, sitting in the same pew every Sunday, and I did not feel comfortable fully sharing my experiences and my problems with the people there. This seems a shame. I don't want to disparage anyone, but it seems like Christians do not always love one another as Christ commanded (John 15:12–14).

My life is not the same as someone else's. I would guess neither is yours. The home church is a group of people who have come together because we believe in Christ, the Bible, and the inevitability of human suffering and death, among other things. But we have no official dogma, and we can share experiences and ideas that are too uncomfortable to talk about in any of the church buildings where I have attended. We read and enlighten each other, using the Bible as our guide, with the help of the Holy Spirit of God.

As we have each suffered in our own lives, we support each other with prayer and compassion. We do not hold ourselves out as "better" or boast of anything. Faith is a gift. God grants gifts to each according to His plan. We rely on Him to give us what we need in the right time to do whatever He commands. I pray for a part to play and courage to play it.

19. ANGELS

Another wonderful thing happened in my life. I found out about angels in the world. The Bible talks about angels, archangels, seraphim, cherubim, The Angel of the Lord, and the Heavenly Host.

I am talking about people, whom I believe God places in our paths for all kinds of reasons. He who sees all and knows all things, reaches into our lives most often, I believe, through people. Like the doctor who prayed for me. It is just something God does.

As I was going up to the cancer center, a two hour drive, I stopped for coffee at a McDonald's. I always stop at the same one or two places, where the food might not be inspiring, but it will not be poisonous either. You cannot be too careful. As I was finishing up, I overheard two people talking who, from what I heard I think were either ministers or at least active church members. In my car I just kept getting a strong feeling to stop and go in and talk to them. Finally, I did. I told them I had overheard that they were Christians, and they said yes, they were. I explained that I was on my way to the cancer center for testing and asked that they pray for me. We three held hands and they said a prayer for me. I still do not know why that particular thing happened, for my sake or theirs, but it did make me feel better. Whether that was the ultimate purpose, I don't know. Sometimes that is the way it is.

Recently, I was in the courthouse. I was very early, because I had wanted to make sure I got a parking place. Then the traffic lights all lined up so I got there faster than usual. The office for Alternate Dispute Resolution was not open yet. I was alone on the fourth floor of this magnificent building. I decided to get in some steps. I have a step counter in my phone. A very modern convenience.

The courthouse is a huge square with a courtyard in the center. The four sides are easily several hundred steps around the whole thing. As I walked I was thinking and hoping I would be doing God's will that day. At a few minutes before time for the office to open, I saw a well-dressed lady sitting on a wooden bench outside the office. I asked if she were there for mediation, and she said yes, she was. I introduced myself and she stood to shake my hand. I said, "You don't have to stand for me." She replied, "Yes, I do. I had twelve years of Catholic school."

I sat down with her and we were conversing. She mentioned she was caring for her father with Alzheimer's, and trying to help her son, who lived on his own, but, had had some sort of trouble in his life. The son was upset that his grandfather had to suffer so much. I said, "God uses our suffering to prepare us for the kingdom." She got tears in her eyes and said, "Can I hold your hand?" I said sure. She took my hand and told me she believed the same, but rarely found anyone she could talk to about it. We sat like that and talked until it was time to go inside. I'm certain that God meant for this to happen.

One time as I went into the same office, early as usual, I met a man who was saved in prison, whom Christ had spoken to in his cell. He was now a minister, leading others to Him. I told him I'd recently had a similar experience. We shook hands and called one another "brother."

Since I was saved, things like this happen all the time. I now expect them to pop into my life when I am not looking for them. I pray to be ready. If you are not ready, you can miss them.

The last day of the winter program at the shelter, one of the men I was concerned about was there. This is a huge, powerfully built fellow that has a shaved head and tattoos going all the way up, the way some former prisoners do. I don't know for sure if he had been one, or if so, his offenses. I never ask, and most do not volunteer the information. I don't really need to know. God's mercy is for all, and so is shelter from the elements. We had made friends over several weeks. I told him I wanted to say goodbye and hoped I would see more of him over the summer. This fellow got tears in his eyes.

He said "You been good to me. Bless you, man." *I believe all blessings come from God, no matter who says them.*

I also know at least two people who wintered at the shelter were saved. One was a man with a terrible drinking problem. He received a spot in a live-in Christian program for men the day he was baptized. Another is around and about, working and seemingly doing well. I see him around from time to time. God bless.

I believe when these things happen, God is letting me know He is there, and He is watching and He is pleased. Amen.

20. THORNS

Paul said he had a "thorn" in his flesh, he prayed for God to take it out, but God would not because it kept him humble (2 Cor. 12:7–10).

I also have thorns. My surgery was August 1, 2016. I have had incontinence since then, I have to carry supplies and stay close to bathrooms. It has curtailed some of the activities I previously enjoyed. It is awkward, embarrassing and humbling.

And of course there is the cancer. For most of 2017 and 2018, the cancer was dormant. This was a huge blessing. The PSA stayed in the lowest range and we even began to hope it would remain there. Even after the androgen deprivation therapy was stopped, the PSA stayed out of sight. I had over two years of no treatment at all. I was planning a procedure to improve the incontinence, so life could get back to "normal."

God's plan was different. Maybe He wants me to remain as I am. His wisdom is beyond my understanding. I trust Him. What does it mean to "surrender" anyway?

I must trust Him, accept His judgment. This body of flesh is a temporary dwelling for the spirit. Paul describes it as a clay jar, a temporary house, and even a tent. Salvation means we have an existence that *transcends* the flesh (1 Cor. 15:42–49). See John 6:40–44.

Thus with trepidation and trembling, I go back to my next testing and expect that I will undergo additional treatment. The doctors believe the metastasis is in my bones. My blood shows that the cancer is growing. The life of all flesh is in the blood (Lev. 17:11). Cancer is a form of life, a mutation from human cells, a change in DNA derived from us, but not exactly us. The army of rebellious cells that have deviated from God's design live, grow and multiply. There is war within my body, and I have no choices but to fight or surrender. God wants us to surrender to Him, not to cancer.

In any event, I do not know when or how I will die any more than anyone else. We need to know that the body dies, because that knowledge brings spiritual growth and transformation. We do not need to know the details, as that is God's domain. I walk boldly upright. *Cancer has not brought me despair, it brought me salvation!*

My worldly sufferings, even the mistakes, have brought me home, to the place I needed to be. My wanderings and searching eventually brought me together with my soulmate. That union gave me my sons, beloved and cherished all the more because I had them later in life. The loss of a kidney and nearly dying brought me to one of my spiritual mentors and eventually to the home church, where I have learned so much and grown spiritually. The fact that I had cancer and was facing the reality of death and the weight of my past sins led me to a vision of the Risen Christ, and to the relief of lifelong burdens of guilt. This in turn led me to the service of the poor, the addicted, and the homeless. The entire experience made it possible for me to love, *really* love God *and* my neighbor. And finally, I have come to the peace of living in submission to Him.

And I am hopeful, that this experience and vision can be shared and help others. I would be truly blessed also if there are others who have had similar visions and dreams and are emboldened and encouraged to come forward and share, as I was reluctant to do. I hope the more people do so, the more others will believe and be saved.

So cancer was used by God as a tool to save me, and *through me He could use it to save others*. This gives all my suffering from cancer and other things a meaningful place in His plan. *We do not suffer for nothing!*

21. LUKEWARM

Laodicea was a Greek town and the location of one of the original churches, which were addressed in the Book of Revelation, chapters 2–3. It was known for the manufacture of ophthalmic medication. It was a prosperous town; people there were well-off. From the text, it is easy to see its problem. Christians there had grown complacent and self-satisfied. They are giving lip service, but not going out into the world carrying the Message of Christ, not sacrificing for the sake of the poor, or taking up their own crosses and following His example. They are boastful about their worldly wealth (Rev. 3:17). The Lord states:

> *"I know your deeds, that you are neither cold nor hot.*
> *I wish you were either one or the other! So, because*
> *you are lukewarm-neither hot nor cold-I am about*
> *to spit you out of my mouth."* (Rev. 3:15–16, NIV)

What is Yeshua (Jesus) saying? The people there are not terribly evil. They are not overtly oppressing the poor, they are not stealing and murdering and fornicating. But they are rich in material things. They are too comfortable. *"I counsel you to buy from me gold refined in the fire, so you can become rich"* (Rev. 3:18).

Gold and silver are refined by fire. The dross (part of the raw ore that is not metal) is thrown out. What is left is valuable. Wheat is sifted and the chaff is burned. People need to be tested and refined for the kingdom. *Our worldly suffering in life is the way God accomplishes our purification.* In my case, at this point, this has come in the form of cancer. But who knows? If I live long enough, perhaps I will be tested in other ways. It does not matter what the test is. The issue is my response.

When Christ was on the cross, nailed to it hand and foot, He forgave His executioners. When the thief on one of the other crosses believed, Jesus saved the thief. His mind was not set on getting away, or on His pain, or on the unfairness of Him dying for us, or on the shame of being executed as a criminal, hung up naked before the world. Instead, He was still full of grace, thinking of others. Think of that. Even in extremis, He thought of other people first, himself last. *"So, the last will be first and the first will be last."* (Mt. 20:16). Yeshua (Jesus) served breakfast to the disciples on the beach before ascending into Heaven (Jn. 21:11–13). He washed their feet at the last supper (Jn. 13:5–16). He prayed for them in the garden (Jn. 17:6–19). By the way, He also prayed for *us* (Jn. 17:20–23). Think of that. Grace.

My prayer is to have grace, even a little of it, a tiny portion, to think of others first, myself last, even in time of trouble and suffering. This, to me, *is* the kingdom of heaven, manifested in our lives. This is the fulfillment of the greatest commandment, the golden rule, the Sermon on the Mount, the sacrifice Paul spoke about, and the law God is writing on our hearts in Jeremiah 31:33.

Christ is speaking to twenty-first century Americans as well as the church at Laodicea. We are fabulous, rich beyond any other people who ever lived on the planet. But we are largely insulated from the suffering of the world. War, plague and famine never touch us directly, except the military and first responders. The persecution of Christians in the Middle East or China never threatens us.

Famously, Richard and Sabina Wurmbrand[4] prayed for a cross to bear, and thereafter were arrested and tortured by the Romanian communist secret police. Richard was tortured for fourteen years, and bore scars on his body that lasted the rest of his life. The fact that we don't have these things in twenty-first century America does not mean we will not have a cross to bear. It may be a reversal of fortune, an accident, or our children's lives, but we will have thorns and burdens and suffering one way or another. This is why I think we need to pray for grace.

---

[4] If you don't know who they are, look it up. You will find out some amazing things!

22. A Cause to Die For

God is always working on us, growing us in spirit, molding us. Our bodies are like jars of clay (2 Cor. 4:7). We are treasures inside jars of clay. Clay pots break in the end, but the treasure isn't lost. The jar is expendable. We are all wasting away, but the spirit is *renewed day by day* (2 Cor. 4:16). Our "light and momentary troubles" are achieving for us eternal glory! (2 Cor. 4:17).

Cancer brought home for me the fragility and temporary nature of this life. But if this life is temporary, so is our suffering. Yes, we suffer, but if we can endure, the suffering will stop.

The generation of the 1930s and '40s lived through the Depression *and* WWII. They suffered and accomplished incredible things. After surviving that, they reasonably wanted safety, comfort, and a better time for their children than they had had. Safe, comfortable and secure. But that plan doesn't take into account the nature of youth. Youth is exploratory, youth is adventurous. Youth is rebellious. These are natural for all young people. They want to take risks; they crave adventures!

The WWII generation had a cause and saved the world. But they wanted their children to go to college and get a management job, or a sales job. Young people want something they can be passionate about, and if it isn't there they tend to create it for themselves.

I think this is why communists like Saul Alinsky have appeal to the young.[5] They give them a cause, something to be passionate about, something to fight for. The problem is it needs to be the right cause. Man cannot save the world on his own, by his own efforts, by his own ideas. Man is the creation, God is the Creator!

---

[5] Alinsky dedicated his book to Lucifer!

Christ has given us a cause and it is one that is good in *every* generation. It is unfortunate that so many churches have not addressed it that way. Church organizations get a special tax break from the government, so that no matter how much money they take in, they don't pay tax. Churches don't want to offend anyone because they have to fill the pews. They collect a lot of money from regular tithes, offerings, capital campaigns, and dinners. They put on bake sales, festivals, and many other money-making enterprises.

They keep the services for the most part uneventful. Occasionally they will have a holiday pageant, or a youth service. They have great music, professional music directors and organists, expensive choir robes, grand pianos and German-made organs, youth ministers, and beautiful buildings.

Did Yeshua go around doing any of these things? No. What about Paul? Paul came to town preaching Christ crucified, a stumbling block to Jews and foolishness to gentiles! Paul was not always well received (1 Cor. 1:23). The man without the spirit does not accept the things that come from the Spirit of God, as they are foolishness to him and he cannot understand them (1 Cor. 2:14).

What did Yeshua tell us to do in this life?

He commanded us to love one another (Christians) *as He loved us.* (Jn. 15:12)

He asked us to care for the poor. (Mt. 25:40)

He told us to forgive other people. (Mt. 6:14)

He told us not to let the cares of the world come between us and God. (Lk. 8:11–15)

Against such things, there is no law. (Gal. 5:22–23)

23. SACRIFICE

In ancient times, when God gave Moses the law, the Hebrews used to sacrifice animals to atone for sin. See Leviticus chapters 1–6. When I first studied this seriously, I could not understand it. How was it different from some pagan ritual that might be performed by naked savages dancing around a campfire in the night? How could anyone be enlightened by such a thing? What does God the Creator want with this blood?

The Hebrew sacrifices were different. A savage thinks the blood pleases his idol or deity. God is not in love with the blood of bulls and rams (Isaiah 1:11). A pagan believes he is paying for a better crop, a transactional exchange, or buying off anger.

The Hebrews had *a special relationship* with the Creator of the Universe. They entered a Covenant, where He agreed to be their God, and they agreed to be His people. He gave the rules and they did their best to follow. Whenever one failed, he essentially broke the covenant. Blood was required, because blood represents life. The penitent placed his hand on the animal in a spirit of repentance, and knowing the innocent animal was standing in for himself and his own blood. The purpose was not to please God with more animal blood. The purpose was to restore the fractured *relationship* of the covenant. Further, it had to be a perfect, unblemished year old male animal. A thing of great value. Like your prize bull. The penitent must feel the loss. It could not be taken lightly.

The blood offerings however, were not just symbolic. First, they were valuable animals. Also they were alive, and the penitent had to kill them himself in the temple. It was far more dramatic than a mere symbol.

Yeshua's death on the cross was the once-for-all atonement for all of us in His blood, as we have been unable to live up to the perfect life God intended since the fall. Since He was perfect and unblemished in spirit as well as form, He was a perfect sacrifice, acceptable to God. He made Himself a *sin sacrifice* for us all (Rom. 5:21).

If we suffer, and even die for Him, we do nothing He did not already do for us. Though He was raised, He first died the death we all die. And He has promised to raise up the believers at the last day (John 6:40).

Because of what I saw, then, I *know* it is true that Yeshua suffered and died for me. I know that my suffering and death are meant to refine and purify me for His kingdom. I know He really will raise me up at the last day, because He already took away the burden of my guilt and the awful weight I carried, and it has not returned to bother me.

Romans 12:1 tells us to make a sacrifice of our bodies, as a spiritual act of worship. We are "members" of the body of Christ (v. 5). We are given various spiritual gifts so that we can all perform different functions, so that the body is complete (v. 6). We are therefore called to live as the embodiment of the one who gave His body for us.

Because I saw and I believe what I saw, I can testify. I am not testifying to hearsay, but to the evidence of my own eyes. I am not seeking anything worldly from this, neither money nor acclaim. Further, *I confess that I do not deserve anything.* If I had the wages I had earned, I would be dead in my sins. I received this vision as a gift because I think it was the only way to save me, I was lost and now I am found, was blind, and now I see. *The hero of this story is Yeshua.* I am just the narrator, led by the inspiration of the Holy Spirit.

I feel compelled by the Holy Spirit to offer this to you, the reader. I've said things in this telling I'd rather not have put into print. I have no choice, because I have hope that by telling these things, you will see that I'm telling the truth. I pray that this helps someone, or multiple people believe more deeply in Jesus Christ, and believe that He is the one and only Son of God Most High, who was sent here not to condemn, but to save people like me *and you.*

I prayed and sought for a long time to have true faith, a belief that was more than hope, more than words. I would have you share that.

I need to warn you. There will be servants of the enemy, the devil, and people for various reasons, who will argue that the experience I had was "only in my head" and I cannot prove anything. Isn't God also the God of my head? If this is in my head, which I don't deny, then God put it there. (They do this out of envy, pride, and other sinful emotions that are put in them by Satan.)

24. Angry People

Communists, atheists, and false believers can get really agitated when you tell them you are saved, that you have found eternal life or met Jesus in a vision. They have their own religion, communism, or atheism. They all have their own doctrines. They all feel an instant need to defend themselves by attacking you. Personally, I think at least some of those attacks come from the devil, the father of lies (John 8:42–47, NIV). The devil does not like competition.

There are philosophers who equate Heaven and Hell with the imaginings of a person who is kept in a cave, and since he cannot see outside the cave, and has no way to test his thoughts, he uses his mind to imagine the way the outside of the cave might be. However, just because I imagine there *is* an outside world does not negate the fact that an outside world exists. The same is true of Heaven. I do not claim to know all the details, and I try not to guess about them. I will find out when God determines that I should.

Some people claim that the Universe was all created in a "big bang" 13.7 billion years ago. I cannot disprove that. But what existed before that? None that I know of can tell us. So I question: the entire universe suddenly sprang forth out of the void, or from a "singularity,"[6] and became the heavens and the earth, and they do not see that there is a place for God in that? In a system that calls itself science, and posits a cause for everything, they cannot provide a cause for the most spectacular event that ever happened, according to their own theory. This does not prove them wrong. But if they proved

---

[6] The "singularity" means all the matter and energy in the universe collected in one massive object.

tomorrow that it happened that way, I would certainly think God was behind it.

What if the universe is billions of years old, and contains trillions of galaxies, each with hundreds of billions of stars? Wouldn't that simply mean that God is bigger and more spectacular than we can even imagine? The awesomeness of the universe simply magnifies the awesomeness of its Creator.

What I can say from my own experience is that when unbelievers, communists and atheists argue against "religion" (really they are arguing against the existence of God), the first places they turn are the theory of evolution and the Big Bang theory. They, *just like my father all those years ago*, point out the various discoveries tending to show that the world is much more than six thousand years old.

What I am saying is that, *compared to the saving grace of God*, offered through the blood of Yeshua, to those who believe in Him, and the fact that God raised Him from the dead, *which is the more important to us?* Believe what you want about the cosmic events, but for Jesus's sake, and the sakes of the un-saved, who might yet be saved, do not let these arguments be used to discourage others' belief in Christ's salvation! I grew up with this argument and became immune to it, but that isn't true for everyone.

The other thing I would say is that the Christians I know do not live in caves. We go out into the real world, we serve the poor. Some Christians even take the Gospel into places (Communist China, Iran) where the powers of the world forbid it to go on pain of death. They sow the seeds of the kingdom. Many of them suffer torture and death, but they do not hold back. They are not the ones in a cave. Academia is the cave; communist China is the real world, and the masters there punish with real pain and physical death. And many Christians have testified to real miracles happening in these places, because the Holy Spirit goes with them, guides them and protects them.

The devil foments unceasing evil activity. There was a report of a group now operating, connected only by the internet, promoting killing, and even mass killing, as sport, keeping scores. There was also recently a report of an academic in one of the Scandinavian countries advocating eating dead people as a way to "save the planet."[7]

So as the Holy Spirit also operates continuously in the world, the devil operates continuously in the world. Both operate mainly through people. To say this is not so, to me, is either naivete' or denial.

Therefore, spiritual warfare is part of life for people who have faith, knowing the devil will try to defeat us at every turn. God didn't save you to have you lose to the minions of the devil. *But you cannot win by yourself.* Just like I couldn't be saved by myself, no matter how hard I *tried*. My trying actually was my downfall, I had to *surrender to Him.* He has the strength, the courage and all the weapons you need.

> *"Finally, be strong in the Lord and His mighty power. Put on the full armor of God so that you can take your stand against the devil's schemes. For our struggle is not against flesh and blood, but against the rulers, against the authorities, against the powers of this dark world and against the spiritual forces of evil in the heavenly realms."* (Eph. 6:10–12)

I believe that is why the Spirit immediately led me to John 5:24, as soon as I had received the vision of Christ. He knows that the devil will try with all his wiles to move me off the path, to deceive me, to take away the saving grace that had been given me.

The fact is I saw, I heard, and I believed. Whatever the reason I saw, whatever the reason I believed, the fact remains that I did. I do. All that remained was to repent and surrender to Him. Which is what I have done, and you can easily do. And when you do, the Holy Spirit will guide you. In fact, Yeshua promised that he would come *and take you by the hand and lead you to the place He is going*! (John 14:1–4, NIV). *He* tells you, not me, *"Do not let your hearts be troubled. You have believed in God; believe also in me."* (Jn. 14:1).

---

[7] All of the devils schemes will fail, God wins. The issue, the reason I wrote this is you and me.

So don't trust me (Joe); trust God and trust Yeshua. Trust the Holy Spirit, who will come and show you all things (Jn. 14:26).

Some people argue about which translation of the Bible one reads from. Without disparaging anyone, to me they all mean the same thing. The wording is slightly different. There is nothing about the KJV that is special except that it was the first English translation, and therefore has become spread throughout the world, because English is the language of the most dominant countries in the past four hundred years. But it was transcribed in the English that was spoken in 1611, which is almost unreadable to modern people. The NKJV is familiar, to those who grew up with it, so it may be special to you. I tell you in sincerity, I believe the inspiration that really matters is what happens *to the person who reads it, as opposed to the person who translated it.* That is the real magic, just in my opinion. You will get from it what the Holy Spirit intends, if you are open to it, and if you let the Holy Spirit be your guide.

Therefore, all arguments against us fail, and do not negate our salvation, because the *work* of our salvation *was done by Yeshua*, not by us. Ours is a salvation by grace, through faith, not by works. If one looks to Christ and believes in Him, he is invited to the banquet, no matter what any human being says (Jn. 6:40). In fact, the harder they argue against us, the more they prove we are really with Yeshua. The devil has no reason to fight so hard against ordinary human foolishness, but he will fight with all he has to undermine real belief and true testimony.

The Holy Spirit, taking me to scripture, knew *exactly* where to point me so that no one can ever take my faith away by human arguments.

> *"For I am convinced that neither death nor life, neither angels nor demons, neither the present nor the future, nor any powers, neither height nor depth, nor anything else in all creation, will be able to separate us from the love of God that is in Christ Jesus, our Lord"* (Ro. 8:38–39).

Paul also spent a lot of time lecturing people not to judge others on debatable matters (Rom. 14:1). In Paul's day, apparently, eating meat and keeping various special days were controversial matters (Rom. 14:2–8). Paul states he believes no food is unclean in itself (Rom. 14:14). But if it bothers a person whose "faith is weak," then you should not eat it, so as not to injure the other's faith (Rom. 14:15). *"The kingdom of God is not a matter of eating and drinking, but of righteousness,* joy and peace *in the Holy Spirit..."* (Rom. 14:17 [my own emphasis]). So be convinced in your own mind and keep it between yourself and God (Rom. 14:22).

I, personally, am of the opinion that the debate of the age of the earth is such a "debatable matter." Unbelievers, atheists and others on Facebook are constantly challenging people's faith with "gotcha" questions related to this and similar subjects. Well-intentioned Christians play into their hands, in my opinion. I tell people with this type of criticism that I am only witness to a vision of the Risen Lord. However, I was not a witness to the Creation, and while I may have beliefs about that, I cannot swear that they are the exact way it happened. I fully believe the opening words of the Bible, *"In the beginning, God created the heavens and the earth"* (Gen. 1:1).

Therefore, I refrain from taking sides in the "young earth-old earth" debate, because I do not want to detract from the power of the witness the Lord *gave* to me.

I did not earn the right to be a witness for Christ. Rather, it was given to me, a poor sinner, as a free gift.

> Where then is boasting? It is excluded. Because of what law? The law that requires works? No, because of the law that requires faith. (Ro 3:27)

25. His Way

I also do not know the answer to the debates about free will and predestination. The Bible says there is predestination, I believe the Bible. It is obvious from the fall, that there is also free will. How do those two things work together? Scholars and theologians from Aquinas to Kierkegaard have debated this. We had to read excerpts from them in college philosophy class. I do not know the answer, but I am drawn to the stories of two guys named Joe. Actually, not exactly "Joe," but rather Job and Jonah.

Job, the story goes was righteous, and trusted God. The devil, Satan, wagered that he could break Job and get him to renounce God, and God took the bet. Job was sorely tested by the devil, lost everything. His home, land, wealth, family. All lost, but he would not renounce (or "curse") God. He had true faith, and trusted and obeyed, no matter what the devil did. He stayed true to the end. In the end, because of his faith, everything was returned to him double (Job 42:10).

Jonah was the opposite type. God personally told him to do something. Specifically go to Nineveh and tell them to repent. Jonah feared to go there and resisted and fled from God. His ship was destroyed in a storm, and he was swallowed by a fish or sea monster, and dwelt in its belly for three days. Eventually the fish spit him out on the beach. When he recognized he couldn't fight God or run away from God, he repented and did what he was told (Jonah 2:10–3:10). God wins in both stories.

Job did it God's way from the start, and in the end, God took care of him. Jonah tried to do things his own way, and in the end he found God too great, and that he had to submit to God's will anyhow. God was merciful. (God, 2; devil, 0.)

Adam and Eve could have not listened to the serpent, could have gone God's way. Personally, I think God always knew that, with the tasty knowledge of good and evil being right there, that the devil would tempt them and they would give in. In any case, God still wins.

As Paul states: *"Therefore, just as sin entered the world through the one man, and death through sin, and in this way death came to all people, because all sinned..."* (Rom. 5:12, NIV). BUT *"if the many died by the trespass of the one man, how much more did God's grace and the gift that came by the grace of the one man, Jesus Christ, overflow to the many"* (Ro. 5:15). (NIV).

So from my layman's point of view, the story of Jonah parallels the story of the fall and the redemption of man.

The parable of the prodigal son is similar. It is one of my favorites, because I identify with the main character, due to my previous life, and the things I needed pardon for. I squandered my first opportunity to become the righteous man I was meant to be by leaving the mainstream church. But I was eventually beaten down and bedraggled, and God made sure I knew all I had done wrong.

But in the parable, the faithful brother was angry because he saw the prodigal being accepted, who had been unfaithful, getting rewarded with a celebration, though he, who had been faithful, had not (Luke 15:29–30). The father was overjoyed because the younger son had come back. He who had been dead was alive (Luke 15:31–32).

So does man have free will? Yes.

Is God sovereign over all things, using all for His purpose? Yes.

Is there redemption for the sinner who repents? Yes.

> *For the Son of God, Jesus Christ, who was preached among you by us—by me and Silas and Timothy—was not "Yes" and "No," but in him it has always been "Yes." (2 Cor. 1:19)*

I am eternally grateful that God does not require us to resolve all these intellectual problems to be saved. In fact, we have to be careful not to overthink it, and become proud in our knowledge and wisdom, and get "puffed up" by thinking we are anywhere near as smart as God. No one may boast before God, and to get cocky could be a person's fatal flaw.

Like everything in the Bible, these stories encourage us to take the better road and trust God, remaining faithful because we trust Him completely in all things. It is hard. People are subjected to far worse things than any I have experienced. Ask the veteran who had three limbs blown off in Iraq. I am not extraordinary. I think the value of my experience is that *I am ordinary, but God still did something* extraordinary *for my salvation!*

So what I know for sure is that Jesus Christ is real. I know God raised Him from the dead. He died for my sins, He took my sins and freed me with His blood on the cross. I believe that the Holy Spirit wants me to testify to this. So I had to write this testimony.

> *If you declare with your mouth, "Jesus is Lord," and believe in your heart that God raised him from the dead, you will be saved.* Ro. 10:9

If you have doubts, if death is knocking at your door, if you need a boost, I pray that you will believe what I have told. I pray that if you read the passages I have referenced and others in your favorite Bible, that they will strengthen you. I pray that the peace and joy that I received will also come to you and that you will grow closer to Him.

Amen.

POSTSCRIPT

This morning I took a walk with my wife in our neighborhood, holding hands as is our custom. It is early autumn, a few trees are starting to turn. The sky is crystalline blue, crisscrossed with the white contrails of jet planes from the airport, silently streaking the sky. The first streaming rays of the sunrise turn dewdrops to dazzling jewels, blazing with rainbow colors. The grass and leaves reflect a thousand shades of green. The sidewalk is full of shimmering light and its reflective elements flash bits of brilliance. There are insects buzzing and chirping in the shrubbery. The birds are singing their songs, each according to its kind. Crows and geese sound overhead. A vulture glides high up.

This is life, God's miracle, in all its inherent beauty. I am light because I am not weighed down by the past. I can take my time because I am not frightened of the future.

My love is by my side. We help and guide each other as we walk. We share our thoughts with our morning coffee.

This is the gift of salvation, the kingdom of God. We are in the present and ready to do whatever God wants us to do. I don't know if I will live a day, a week, or a decade. It doesn't matter. I know I have been resting in His hands the whole way, long before I was aware of it.

Of course we are fully aware that this idyllic existence is for now, this brief moment in time. We do not ask for it to continue forever. We eagerly await His calling, and we are anticipating and making ready for whatever He might want us to do.

The grace of Jesus Christ was always right there for me, but, like that time at camp when I went into the pool before I learned to swim, I couldn't understand that all I had to do was touch my toes to the bottom and look up, and I was saved; I could breathe. This, I think, is where we are much of the time. If we just reach up, and take His hand, we will be saved. So my closing prayer is for everyone to see that and do it.

Blessings.

ABOUT THE AUTHOR

Joe McGee is a retired trial lawyer living in the Cincinnati area, with his wife of forty-four years and two cats. He has two grown sons and lives an active life, despite having cancer. He does volunteer mediation for the Hamilton County, Ohio, court and volunteers at a homeless shelter. He worships God with Christian friends in a home church. He and his wife are frequently seen in the neighborhood walking and holding hands.